# THE PRIESTLY LIFE

# THE PRIESTLY LIFE

*A Retreat*

## RONALD KNOX

Sheed & Ward · New York

Nihil obstat:

Vincent Maloney, S.S.E.
*Censor Delegatus*

January 15, 1958
Imprimatur:

✠Robert F. Joyce, D.D.
*Bishop of Burlington*

January 17, 1958

Manufactured in the United States
of America

# CONTENTS

# THE PRIESTLY LIFE

# 1

## ENERGY AND REPOSE

### I

It was St. Augustine, I think, who first coined that fine phrase about the nature of Almighty God which tells us that he is *semper agens, semper quietus,* always active, yet always at rest. Always active—we can read the assurance of that all around us. The trembling of a leaf, the downward plunge of a waterfall, the flicker of flames on the hearth; all that motion is not self-originated. Look at a fly zigzagging endlessly between the floor and the ceiling; all that capacity for motion is not merely implanted in it but imparted to it from moment to moment from without. And we too, with all our freedom of choice, are not sufficient explanation of the life that beats in us. All the activity in the Universe, even if it is mediated by angelic or human creatures, is originated by Almighty God. And all that, even, is only a by-product, a faint echo, as it were, of an eternal pulsation. Before suns or worlds were created, the Three Persons of the Blessed

Trinity exercised, in their mutual relations, the everlasting activity of the divine life.

And yet, *semper quietus*, always at rest. As the bush that Moses saw on Mount Horeb burned continually yet was not consumed, so in God, who is pure Act, there is no change of state, no diminution of force, no recovering of wasted energies. When we are told that he rested the seventh day after the work of creation, that is only a metaphor, only an analogy. While he created the whole hierarchy of the angels, the whole system of the heavens, that activity could never alter for a moment his eternal, inviolable repose.

The divine perfections are mirrored for us, as completely as the conditions of humanity allow, in the human nature and mortal life of our Lord Jesus Christ. That, after all, is one of the great reasons for the Incarnation; by reason of it we can read the mysteries of the Divine Nature translated, so to say, into human language. And here too you will find that the two qualities I have mentioned existed simultaneously, though they could not be exhibited simultaneously. All through his ministry he is cramped for time; he is in such a hurry to complete the work his Father has given him to do that he has no leisure even to eat, as he preaches to the thronging multitudes, and when he would pray, he must withdraw to a mountain and spend in prayer the hours while the rest of the world is asleep.

We are accustomed to divide that Life, and quite rightly, into two sections—the hidden life of thirty years, when he dwelt at Nazareth and was obedient to Our Lady and to his foster-father St. Joseph, and the public life of less than three years' duration, when he went about doing good. But we should do wrong if we thought of those thirty years as years of mere quiescence, or of those three years as years of restless activity. During his hidden life he was at work in the carpenter's shop, he knew the pinch of poverty and the necessity of daily toil. Monotony of occupation, a life of drudgery, does not as a rule make for recollection and repose; if it did, I suppose many of us would be in a fair way to becoming saints. Yet during all those years in Our Lord's hidden life there was no stroke of the hammer, no screech of the saw, which was not accompanied by a perfect interior act of oblation. And in his public life, though the multitude thronged about him, and his feet tired on the roads and at night he had not where to lay his head, always he was consciously in the presence of his Heavenly Father, always he was enjoying that presence in a manner which the most highly privileged among his saints never dreamed of.

For the theologians teach us that Our Lord, as Man, was *simul viator et comprehensor*: he lived in our world, and at the same time he enjoyed, even as man, that full and open vision of God which is to be man's reward in heaven. We cannot begin to understand such a conception; but it is theologically certain that while he lay in the manger at Bethlehem, stretching out his hands in helpless infancy to his Virgin Mother, while he hung upon the Cross, every muscle wearied out with the strain of his agony and every joint racked with suffering, he was even then enjoying in that secret fastness the open vision of God. Our Lord was, all his life, at one with the Church Militant and simultaneously at one with the Church Triumphant. *Semper agens*—there was no incident of mortality, sin only excepted, that he would not experience. *Semper quietus*—he achieved that experience without ceasing to enjoy, even in his human nature, the rest which is the supreme recompense for all human endeavour.

And if we expect to find the Life of God mirrored in the human Nature of Our Lord, so we expect to find his human Nature mirrored in the Blessed Sacrament. Here, too, he is always active, yet always at rest. Always active; from day to day, through the hands of his priests, he offers himself upon a million altars for the world's salvation. Not, indeed, that he can labour or suffer or sorrow any more; that is all over; only once the Agony and the scourging, only once the nails and the lance and the Crown of Thorn. But the force which was generated, if we may so crudely describe it, by the Sacrifice made once for all on Calvary still pulsates and energizes in the Holy Sacrifice of the Altar. The Divine Victim is still at work, fresh graces to be won, fresh needs to be met, fresh sins to be atoned for. Think of a piece of music, that is finished, you might say, once for all when the composer's hand makes the last scratch upon the paper. In a sense, yes, but in a sense it has only just begun; the same piece of music will be played again and again all the world over; the echoes of the original composition will not die, it may be, as long as mankind lasts. So it is with our Lord's sacrifice; in a sense the stab of the lance put the final stroke to it, yet in a sense it has never ceased and never can cease while the world stands. Christ still lives among us, his fellow-men, and because he so lives, he is still at work. We go up to the altar with our hearts full of desires and longings which our conscious thoughts can hardly express; and all these desires and

longings of ours are caught up and whirled away from us
by the continuous stream of intercession which goes up from
the Sacred Heart. It is a great furnace, this Sacrament of the
altar, a great work-shop of prayer; never idle for a moment,
while there are human needs to be met, and human tears
to be wiped away.

Ever active; and yet, ever at rest—if we throw ourselves
down, even for a moment, before the Tabernacle, how deep
is the peace that steals over us; how the unruly motions of
our hearts are stilled; how we can take refuge, as in a sudden
harbour, from the buffetings of worldly circumstance! The
flame that burns in the sanctuary lamp is, we know, a succession of flames, just as much as the ignition of a motor-car;
and yet how stilly it burns! So that Presence, which the sanctuary lamp heralds and honours, is a centre of ceaseless activity, and yet the influence that breathes from it is, for us,
an influence of repose.

Sweet Sacrament of Rest—if you want to know what that
means, you should go to a place like Tyburn Convent in
London, where they have perpetual Adoration within a
stone's throw of the Marble Arch. In summer, especially,
when the windows are open; you can hear the whirring and
grinding and hooting of the cars, the tramp of ceaseless
passers-by along the pavement, the distant echoes of the
Park Orators, preaching a dozen rival creeds to indifferent
London. All that you hear, but you hear it as if it was the
noise of a different world; for where you kneel there is nothing but stillness—the stillness of the two nuns at their post
of adoration, the undying, unflickering flame of the candles,
and beyond that the monstrance with its tremendous Bur-

den of living Silence. Always at rest—hidden beyond the reach of eye or sense, he who reigns so tranquilly in heaven reigns tranquilly here; no motion, no breath betrays the presence of a God. *Semper agens*—in the holy Mass he is still busy with his work of reparation and intercession. *Semper quietus*—in the Tabernacle he enfolds his worshippers with the sense of eternal peace.

The earthly Life of our Blessed Lord is mirrored again, though less perfectly, less unmistakably, in the Life of his Church. The Church is his mystical Body, animated by his own Spirit; we expect, then, to find in her life some echo, some reflection of his. And the Church too, in her own way, is *semper agens, semper quieta*. Always active—her missionaries going out to spread the Gospel in lands which have barely heard of her Master's Name; her theologians still agitated with controversy, her preachers calling upon men to repent; her priests shepherding their flocks and ushering them into eternal life from the cradle to the grave. More than that, she has a part to play in the world; political events affect her position, political movements call for her condemnation or approval; she must ever be on the alert, she must always live at high pressure. Her enemies are ready to call her a busybody and bid her mind her own affairs; but she is wiser than they—and knows that religion cannot be divorced from life; that political movements and currents of philosophical thought must affect, in their degree, the eternal welfare of men's souls. She is always at work, and if you once ask yourself the question, Which of the world's rulers is the busiest? Which of them works the longest hours, and takes the least holiday? you will not take long to find the answer. It is the man in a white cassock who rules without an army, almost without a territory, in the Vatican Palace at Rome.

And yet for all this bustle of hers, there is a sense in which the Church is *semper quieta*, always at rest. For if you would know her true self, if you would approach near to the innermost secret of her life, you must go, not to the palaces of Pope or bishop, not to the courts of ecclesiastical tribunals, or the lecture rooms of learned theologians. You must go to the cells of Carthusians and Carmelites, of Trappists and Poor Clares, if you want to know what the Church really is. Shut off from the noise of the world and its dusty disputes, sheltered by their protecting walls from public inquisitiveness and from the blare of advertisement, these cloistered souls find an interior peace which is, if we would but realize it, the breath of the Church's Life, the source of her triumphs, the solace of her despairs. Look at a man or a horse racing; and then remember that behind all that tremendous display of outward activity there is one tiny valve which beats all unseen, all unheard, within the breast; and if that beating were to cease, all the external activities would cease with it. Something of the same importance belongs to those homes of silence and recollectedness where men and women serve God in holy religion: there lies the heart of the Church. Their restfulness is her secret life; the power-house from which all her restless activity must spring. Go elsewhere, and you will see the rippling of her muscles; it is in the hours of contemplation that you will hear the beating of her heart.

## II

*Semper agens, semper quietus*—such is the Life of Almighty God, the direct Agent in all change, all motion, all becoming, yet himself unchanged, unmoved, uninfluenced. *Semper agens, semper quietus*—such was the Incarnate Life of Jesus Christ, when he went about as Man, toiling and suffering for our sakes, yet never losing for a moment the interior peace which they enjoy who see God face to face. *Semper agens, semper quietus*—such is the Life of Jesus Christ in the Blessed Sacrament; offering himself day by day as a spotless oblation, atoning for our fresh sins and winning us fresh graces, yet, in the Tabernacle, the Type and the Source of rest. *Semper agens, semper quieta*—such, in its degree, is the life of Holy Church, always restlessly at work over her business of world-conquest, yet ever finding repose in the hidden lives of her contemplative children. And now, what of your life and mine?

Is it too much to say that our lives ought to be modelled on the same pattern, ought to bear the same hallmark, ought to have this double character of energy and repose? If we are really to understand our Christian vocation, that *semper agens, semper quietus* ought to be our motto too. Always active; we cannot afford to stand still. Apart from the press of our secular business, our home duties, our duty to the nation in a time of peril, the need of making a livelihood, and so on, we have to work out our own salvation, we are told—the devil is only too ready to take advantage of us if he sees us trying to mark time. And yet, always at rest. Why else does the epistle to the Hebrews imply that we have already entered into rest by becoming Christians? Why does the Sacred Heart say "Come unto me, and I will give you rest"? There is a rest, even here, for the people of God; there is, for every soul which has really learned to love our Blessed Lord and to abide in his love, a fortress of interior peace which no assault from the world can enter, no echoes of the world's anxieties disturb. The soul which has learned to practise the presence of Christ, and to be happy alone with him, has found something more than peace in heaven; it has found peace on earth. That is how the Saints lived; that is how they contrived to undertake such vast labours, such heroic mortifications. "You are dead" St. Paul writes, "and your life is hidden with Christ in God". If we only believed that, if we only understood that! Then indeed we should be able to face the worst life has in store for us with careless eyes. You are a good active Christian? Thank God. And now, since he has given you the grace to be active in his service, ask one more grace of him; ask that you may learn of him, learn of the Sacred Heart, how to rest quietly in his love.

You see, we're so accustomed to divide our life into alternations of activity and quiescence; we work and then we rest and then we work and then we rest; what other arrangement is possible? And I suppose that most of us, when we think of our retreat, think of it by a sort of pious metaphor as a spiritual holiday; at other times of the year we are too busy to think as much about God as we would like to; now we are at leisure to be, for once, our true selves.

Perhaps it is simplest to put it in this way; that we ought to try and expunge one phrase from our vocabulary as far as possible; I mean the phrase "going out of retreat". We oughtn't, if you will excuse my saying it, to go into retreat with the feeling that later on we are going out of it, like a man doing a treatment at a spa in the hope that afterwards he will find it has done him some good. We ought to be more like invalids who are just preparing to get up, and are having a course of massage for their legs so that when they do get up they will be able to walk. We are trying to gain, in this week, a poise of the soul which will, please God, remain ours. And we shall have succeeded, in proportion as his grace enables us, when we have "come out of retreat", to live in greater recollection than before; always active, because even our times of recreation will be filled with a desire of living in his glory; always at rest, because the most exhausting labours will never be able to distract our attention, entirely, from him.

What is it, in its own nature, the habit of recollection? It doesn't mean merely pulling yourself up and thinking seriously about your state of life, your duties, your sins, your temptations, your ambitions, and the rest of it. Recollection doesn't mean thinking about "your" anything; it means thinking about you. Put it in this way—you and I are breathing all day, but unless we are asthmatic we are not conscious of our breathing; we go on doing it without thinking about it. Now direct your attention to the fact that you are breathing, and you become conscious of it at once. You can feel, you can hear yourself breathing. In the same way, we spend most of our lives thinking without thinking about it; the attention of our minds is directed outwards towards the objects of our thought, not inwards towards ourselves think-

ing. Now direct your attention to the fact that you are thinking; you become conscious at once of your own immortal
soul. This thing which is thinking all the time, which is thinking at this moment about itself, is an immortal substance
specially created by God, and destined to survive to all eternity. It is nearer to us than anything else can be. But you
were not thinking about it until I suggested it to you just
now.

In the solitude in which we find ourselves we find God.
Turn your eyes outwards, towards the stars or the ocean or
the sunset, and you will be able to argue God's existence,
but you will not attain to his presence. He *is* present everywhere; but whenever you think of him as present, there will
always be some space, some distance, intervening between
you and him, unless. . . . Unless you turn back upon yourself, and look into your own soul. There you will find him,
with no barrier of space to cut him off, even in imagination, from you. He is present in every operation of your soul;
its thoughts, it memories, its desires, all its activities, exist
only through the powers of motion which he lends to it.
That, even in the natural order; and in the supernatural
order the motions of his grace are playing over your soul all
the time like sunshine over a pool. When you look for the
presence of God, do not worry about *here* and *there*; wherever you are, you have only to look into yourself, and you
will find him.

I wonder if we make a practice of doing that as much as
we ought to, even those of us who are living lives of serious
purpose, and of regular observance? Yet it is such an easy
thing to do; not necessarily in our times of prayer—though

it is the best possible preface to our times of prayer—but at odd moments during the day. You have to wait two or three minutes for an engagement or a 'bus or a train; and your eyes wander at once towards the people who are passing by, or even to the advertisements on the hoardings—what advertisements! Those two or three minutes pass in idle speculation; if you kept your eyes still, and suddenly turned back your thoughts upon yourself, you will find yourself, just for those two or three minutes, in the presence of God. Or you may use even a shorter interval of time; when you are just switching over from one occupation to another, you can pause just for that fraction of time, and look into your own soul, and greet for a moment, as a soldier salutes his senior officer, the presence of God there. The busiest day can be sanctified, if its moments are thus punctuated by the recollection of God in the soul.

Let us be clear about it—no state of life, whatever opportunities of prayer it gives us, however rigid be the framework of observance within which it moves, will guarantee for us, of itself, the habit of recollection. There will always be interests, attachments, ambitions ready to distract our thoughts, and so draw us away from ourselves. There will always be excuses for neglecting ourselves, for hiding ourselves away from God's presence upon the pretext of serving him by our activities. Martha can always put up a good defence against Mary. And, in proportion as we allow that to happen, we are spoiling not only the temper of our spiritual lives but, very often, the effectiveness of our work as well. We shall become fussy, and impatient, and irritable, and despondent, and jealous, and critical and sentimental, and generally unbalanced, and all that will tell—will take away something from our efficiency, will hamper the value of our actions, quite apart from spoiling the purity of our intentions. Our influence on other people will be the less and the poorer, if we have no roots of recollection in ourselves. *Semper agens, semper quietus,* that is the character which will tell. If you miss that, you will be *semper agitans, semper agitatus;* you will live in an atmosphere of tension which you will communicate to others, and so make life less happy and work less fruitful both for them and for you.

So let us ask Almighty God if he will not deepen in us, in the course of this retreat, the spirit of recollection.

# 2

# CREATION AND THE PRIEST

If a man should set out to go through the Bible, pausing and making a meditation wherever he found material, he would be a dull fellow if his attention was not caught by the second verse of it. "The earth was void and empty, and darkness was upon the face of the deep. And the spirit of God moved over the waters." Creation still in the melting-pot; so that we have nothing for our composition of place except a formless sea of undifferentiated matter, dark, not by some effect of shadow, but with that primal darkness that reigned before light was made. And over this inert mass, like the mist that steals up from a pool at evening, moved, already, the Spirit of God. Already it was God's plan to educe from this chaos the cosmos he had resolved to make, passing up through its gradual stages till it culminated in the creation of Man.

Deep in your nature and in mine, as we sit here, lies just such a chaos of undifferentiated matter, of undeveloped potentialities. Psychologists call it, the unconscious. It is a

14

great lumber room, stocked from our past history. Habits and propensities are there, for good and for evil; memories, some easily recaptured, some tucked away in the background; unreasoning fears and antipathies; illogical associations, which link this past experience with that; primitive impulses, which shun the light, and seek to disguise themselves by a smoke-screen of reasoning; inherited aptitudes, sometimes quite unsuspected. Out of this welter of conditions and tendencies the life of action is built up, your life and mine. And still, as at the dawn of creation, the Holy Spirit moves over those troubled waters, waiting to educe from them, with the co-operation of our wills, the entire life of the Christian.

With us, he has set about that business in a special way. He has made us priests; and there is a curious analogy, I think, between the process by which God made man, and the institution of the priesthood. I hope you will bear with me if I draw out that parallel rather in detail.

When did God make man? Why, at the very end of his creation, and (if we may so say without irreverence) by a kind of afterthought. Already he had made, on the sixth day, the beasts of the field; you quite expect to hear, after that, "And there was morning and evening, a sixth day". But no, all was not over yet. God said, "Let us make man, after our own image"—almost as if it were a kind of sudden inspiration, like that of a child inventing a new game: "Let us make man". That puts us in our place rather, doesn't it? To think that God might have been content to make a world in which the plants grew with no human hand to weed or to tend them, a world in which the animals survived or perished according to the law of their nature, with no human master to kill them, or to tame them to his purposes. But at the last moment, God said, "Let us make man".

When did our Lord institute the priesthood? Well, in a sense on Maundy Thursday, on the last evening of his mortal life. But he did not make his intention clear until he met his apostles again on Easter Day in the Cenacle; when he breathed on them and said, "Receive ye the Holy Ghost". Once more, you see, it is a kind of afterthought; the work of our Redemption is finished, death has been vanquished, and hell harrowed, and the holy patriarchs have gone to their reward, and the reign of grace has begun—and our Lord did all that without any priests to help him. He trod the wine-press alone, and of the people there was none with him. And he could have achieved your sanctification and mine, could have spread his gospel through the world and given mankind faith to justify them, charity to sanctify them, without any priests to help him, if he had decreed to do so. But no, at the last moment, a thought seems to strike him, "Let us make priests".

Why did God make man? Partly, no doubt, because he wanted, from his creation, a conscious response of gratitude. When he made sun and moon and stars, and the earth with all its delicate beauty, its intricate workmanship, he pronounced it very good, and the sons of God shouted for joy, we are told, at this new thing that had come to be. But within the material universe itself there was no answering cry of recognition. True, the stars in their courses, the orderly process of the seasons, shewed forth the glory of God; true, the living animals could enjoy some confused pleasures of memory and hope, and in doing so rendered a kind of mute homage to their Creator. But amid all that wealth of multitudinous life no conscious response was given, until he made man, to be, as we say, the priest of creation; to praise God on behalf of those dumb, material things, with a mind that could reason and a voice to express their thankfulness. The priest of creation; the instrument through which the chorus of its praise should thrill and become vocal at last.

But there was more than that; Almighty God wanted his creation to be taken in hand for him. Why, we do not know; but the want is clearly expressed in the account which scripture gives us, "There was not a man to till the ground". God did not make man to be a kind of toy, a final piece of craftsmanship more subtle, more delicate than all the rest. He made him to bear rule over the birds and the beasts and the fishes; to be the viceroy of his new dominion. He was to impose God's will on this planet; he was to be a kind of tool by which God's action would express itself, through the long centuries during which the visible order was to persist.

Why did our Lord institute the priesthood? Partly because he wanted to have a special set of men who would have the freedom and the leisure to make a whole-time job of his service. The rest of us would be so busy, earning our daily bread and looking after our families and fulfilling our various duties as citizens, that we should not be able to attend on him as continually as we should have wished, to think about him as uninterruptedly as we should have wished. Partly that, but partly also because he wanted this new supernatural creation of his, the Christian Church, to be taken in hand for him. As he would have man to look after the dumb beasts, to fold them and guide them and feed them, so he would have priests to look after the faithful, to fold them and guide them and feed them in the ways of the supernatural life. He could have done without us, but he preferred to have, once more, a kind of tool through which his action should express itself. Tools in his hand, that is what we priests were to be.

How did God make man? Doubtless you have to make some allowance for the use of figurative speech; we do not go to the book of Genesis for exact chemical formulae. But when we are told that the Lord God formed man out of the slime of the earth, it surely must mean this, whatever else it means—that man on his physical side is one with the material creation which surrounds him. We may strut and give ourselves airs, and tell one another that we have conquered practically the whole of nature and it is only a matter of time before we conquer the rest of it; but the fact remains, we were made of the slime of the earth; dust thou art, as the priest says to us on Ash Wednesday, dust thou art, and unto dust shalt thou return. If we are anything more than dust, it is only because God saw fit, of his free bounty, to do something else. "God breathed into his nostrils the breath of life, and man became a living soul." That lifeless thing, a mere toy of dumb clay, which lies there on the ground—it is only God's inspiration that has turned it into this wonderful creature we know and are, Man.

How did our Lord institute the priesthood? "When he had said this, he breathed on them, and said, Receive ye the Holy Ghost. Whose sins you remit, they are remitted unto them, and whose sins you retain, they are retained." With one breath, God created the whole human family; with one breath, our Lord instituted the whole Christian priesthood. As man is a beast among the beasts, so the priest is a man amongst men; he shares their passions, their weaknesses, their disabilities. And yet, when God breathes into the face of a priest, a new thing, in a sense, comes into being, just as when God breathed into the face of that clay image he had fashioned. It was a kind of second creation, when our Lord spoke those words in the Cenacle. It brought into the world a new set of powers, infinitely exceeding all that man had ever experienced, all that man could ever expect. It was a fresh dawn of life—supernatural life. Man could no more have evolved into a priest than a beast could have evolved into a man; it was a special creation, this time too.

What is the meaning of all that? It would have been possible, it might even have seemed natural, that our Lord, having won our redemption for us, should apply the fruits of that redemption to our souls without any kind of priestly ministry to aid his purpose. Many who value the name of Christian still find it reasonable to believe that he did just that; the priesthood, they will tell you, belonged to the Jewish covenant, to the old Law; when the mercy of God shone out to us in the face of Jesus Christ, the need for all ceremonies and sacraments was done away. But it is not so that the courtesy of our Lord Jesus Christ treats us. When he turned water into wine at Cana of Galilee, he used no word, no touch, no gesture, to claim the miracle as his own. "Fill the water-pots with water. . . . Draw out now, and bear to the governor of the feast"—the miraculous transformation should take its effect between the hands of the servants who were waiting on the guests; they should have the apparent credit for it. And so it was when he multiplied the loaves in the wilderness. He gave the loaves and fishes to the disciples to distribute; it was in their hands, it seems, that the multiplication took place. It is part of his courtesy, you see, that he will thus associate human agents with himself, just when he gives us the most startling proofs of his miraculous power.

And so it is with the Christian priesthood. Not only when he gives us, under the forms of bread and wine, his own Body and Blood to be our food; in all the Sacraments he is the true author, the true fountain of grace, yet he will suffer a human ministry to intervene. "Receive ye the Holy Ghost; whose sins ye shall remit, they are remitted unto them, and whose sins ye retain, they are retained." But most, and most characteristically, in the Sacrament of Holy Eucharist. When a priest baptizes or absolves, he stands there, sits there, only to unseal the fountains of grace to the faith, to the penitence, which knock to receive them. But when he stands at the altar, the priest does something more; he takes upon himself the Person of Christ, re-enacting in his name the ceremony which he performed on the night of his Passion. A priest clad in the sacred vestments (says the author of the *Imitation*) is the vice-gerent of Christ himself. He uses our Lord's own words, identifies himself with the offering which our Lord continually makes before the Father, of his own Body and Blood. How is it that men can be found with the assurance, with the presumption, to do that?

The difficulty is solved for us by one golden phrase of St.

John Chrysostom's; we all know it. "When you see a priest offering the Sacrifice," he says, "do not think of it as if it were *he* that is doing this; it is the hand of Christ, invisibly stretched forth". The hand of Christ invisibly stretched forth—that is the picture we should conjure up to our minds if we are to think of the Mass as it really is. Aristotle, in defining the position of a slave, uses the words, "A slave is a living tool". And that is what the priest is, a living tool of Jesus Christ. He lends his hands, to be Christ's hands, his voice, to be Christ's voice, his thoughts, to be Christ's thoughts; there is, there should be, nothing of *himself* in it from first to last, except where the Church allows him, during two brief intervals of silence, to remember his own intentions before God. Non-Catholics who come to our churches complain sometimes, don't they, that the ceremonies of the Mass seem so lifeless, so mechanical. But you see, they *ought* to be mechanical. What the visitor is watching, so uncomprehendingly, is not a man, it is a living tool; it turns this way and that, bends, straightens itself, kneels, gesticulates, all in obedience to the orders given it—Christ's orders, not ours. We do not expect eccentricities from a tool, the tool of Christ.

In an ordination ceremony, the future priest is stretched out at full length, face downwards, like a corpse, like a dummy, while the solemn chant of the litany rolls over his head. He is waiting there like a dead thing, for the Holy Spirit to come and quicken him into a new form of life; as Adam's body waited, slime of the earth, for the informing touch of the Creator's hand to turn it into a living soul. He is yielding his body to Christ to be *his* instrument, as if he had no life, no will of his own. And even when he has risen from the ground, his hands must be tied together with a purificator, in token that he is the captive of Jesus Christ; his slave, to drive and control at will. "I live, now not I, but Christ liveth in me"—that is the protestation which these ceremonies make on behalf of the newly-ordained priest. No life of his own, no liberty of his own; henceforth he is Christ's.

This slavery to which the priest commits himself does not begin and end when he is saying Mass, when he is performing ceremonies. Ah, if only it did! No, it is a life-time of service; a life-time during which the priest must consecrate himself, must keep on consecrating himself afresh, to his Master, if only for the sake of the flock which his Master has entrusted to him. The merely mechanical part of a priest's life, the ceremonies he has to perform, the sacred words he has to utter—these come easier to him with use as time goes on. It is not so with the consecration of the heart. That is in danger of growing more formal, more faint, as the love between husband and wife is in danger of growing more formal, more faint, when the bloom has rubbed off their romance. The priest, as the years pass, will be tempted to settle down into a rut, to be satisfied with formal pieties and think he is doing well enough. There will be disappointments, too, and discouragements, to make him cynical and disillusioned. God forgive us, how many of us become crooked tools in the hand of Christ!

Don't let's forget that man was created to live in a Paradise, and lost it through a kind of claustrophobia. Even there, he could wish for wider horizons. Do you remember

the description of how Adam and Eve met their Creator after
the Fall? We are told that the Lord God walked in the Paradise at the afternoon air, and called to them, "Adam, where
art thou?" And they? They had hid themselves away in the
trees of the garden. Do not let us waste time over discussing,
in what sense he who is everywhere present could be said to
walk, at a particular time, in his Paradise; how he, whose
scrutiny is infallible, could need to search for his truant creatures. The picture given us in the book of Genesis is at least
amply borne out by our own experience. Do not we know
what it is to have offended God, to be sought out by God,
and to endeavour, by futile efforts, to hide ourselves away
from that Divine pursuit?

It is what the economists would call, I think, a vicious
spiral. The more we consent to sin, the more we neglect
our prayers, because it would make us uncomfortable to
meet God like that; we should feel ashamed of ourselves—
and besides, we should have to promise amendment. So we
neglect our prayers, and through the neglect of prayer comes
fresh sin. I am not thinking now of mortal sins, I am not
thinking of people who give up prayer altogether. But how
easy it is, when we are being careless about deliberate venial
sin, or about the remote occasions of mortal sin, to funk
meeting God! To take refuge in the love of creatures, or
even—heaven help us, what strange beings we are!—to take
refuge in our work, so long as it is quite external to ourselves, just like Adam and Eve hiding among the trees of
the garden, so as to make certain that we are never left alone
with God. And we become blunt tools, rusted tools, in the
hand of Jesus Christ.

He is looking for you, the tool that once glittered so bright with the oil of consecration. He is looking for you, the lost shepherd. "I never seem to come across him now" you may picture our Lord as saying; "I must see if I can find him at the retreat". At some familiar turn of the walks, consecrated for you, perhaps, by memories of youth, he is waiting for you. In the cool of the afternoon air, when the busy jarring of your daily interests, anxieties, grievances has died down, and there is peace in your heart, he is waiting for you. In some passage of a book you have taken out of the library, a book you have often read before without being specially arrested by that passage, he is waiting for you. There will be a moment of embarrassment, but it need not be more than a moment. You have only to cast yourself down, with Peter, at his knees, and say, with Peter, "Depart from me, for I am a sinful man, O Lord". He will not take you at your word.

# 3

# THE AMBASSADORS OF
# CHRIST

The epistle for the first Sunday in Lent (2 Cor. vi, 1–10), try as we may to make it sound as if it referred to the congregation, refers really to ourselves. It is so plainly St. Paul's conception of what his ideal priest ought to be like.

The Liturgy makes the whole passage somewhat mystifying by leaving out the verses immediately before, which set the key for the whole. "We are Christ's ambassadors, and God speaks to you through us; we entreat you in Christ's name, make your peace with God." St. Paul's metaphor, then, is that of an ambassador, and an ambassador delivering, on behalf of his Sovereign, an ultimatum, a direct threat of war. The priest, at the beginning of Lent, has to entreat his congregation not to offer the grace of God an ineffectual welcome. So many graces missed already, and now the acceptable time has come, the day of salvation; treat this Lent, brethren, as if it was your last chance! Lent, you see, is a kind of sacramental expression of the span of life that still lies before us, the time granted us for repentance, for making our peace with God. If we do not make our peace with God, then, at the expiration of the time fixed, of the days of grace he has offered us, we find ourselves in a state of war with God, his enemies, and eternally. It is an ultimatum we deliver; now or never, make your peace!

So far, the moral has been for the congregation; the rest of the epistle is a moral, entirely, for the priest himself. We are careful not to give offence to anybody, lest we should bring discredit on our ministry; Christ wants for his ambassadors, not just any sort of ambassadors, but ambassadors trained in a school of Divine diplomacy. Not mere towncriers, shouting out "Oyez, oyez!" so as to say, afterwards, that everybody in the street has had fair warning; men entrusted with plenipotentiary powers, to secure the renewed loyalty of the rebellious subjects, if there is any form of persuasion that can do it. It is for the ambassador to ingratiate himself with the people of the country he is sent to; make people love and respect him, so that they may love and respect the master he represents.

To be the ambassador of Christ after a fashion, makes no great demands on the priest. All he has to do is to get up every Sunday morning, read out the Credo, and say "If you don't believe that, my dear brethren, you will go to hell"; get up every Sunday evening, read out the Ten Commandments, and say, "If you don't keep those, my dear brethren, you will go to hell". The ultimatum has been delivered— yes. But have we really been ambassadors? John Wesley, when one of his sermons hadn't made much impression, used to note the fact in his journal, and add, "I am clear of these men's blood". He was a great man, John Wesley, but I don't like him when he uses that phrase. Don't let us ever get into the habit of thinking that after having given our congregation twenty minutes on the danger of mixed marriages, and twenty minutes more on the importance of being in time with the bench rents, we are "clear of their blood". Something more is demanded of an ambassador; what? St. Paul goes on to tell us; not very tidily, because he hadn't a very tidy mind; but perhaps more tidily than usual.

Patience, a great deal of patience—that, he tells us, is the first thing we need. And he goes on to give nine samples of the kind of things we have to put up with, divided into three threes. "In times of affliction, of need, of difficulty"—those are the mental discomforts brought on us by the vicissitudes of our work; "under the lash, in prison, in the midst of tumult"—those are the bodily discomforts inflicted on us by our fellow-men; "when we are tired out, sleepless, and fasting"—those are the bodily discomforts inflicted on us by circumstance. The picture seems to us highly-coloured; do not let us forget that priests in many parts of the world are having, now, to work under those conditions; times may change, and we may have to ourselves. Meanwhile, patience is not less demanded of us because the provocations to which we are accustomed are, by comparison, pin-pricks. How difficult it can be when the faithful *will* try to buttonhole us after Mass on Sunday; when we are tired out after the confessional yesterday, sleepless after mutton-chops at half-past nine and a long evening with the notices, fasting until after the last Mass is sung; in affliction, need, and difficulty because we are already trying to buttonhole so many people ourselves, trying to remember what it is we have so importantly got to say to them; the last moment when we want to be under the lash of the parish grouser, imprisoned by the parish bore, in the midst of tumult, with the altar-boys kicking up a shindy all around us—and this is the moment when, most of all, the parish sees us, and ought to see us at our best!

You don't need to tell me that it is the fault of the laity. Only last Sunday I preached to fifty school girls imploring them not to grow up into the kind of people who buttonhole priests after Mass. But it *is* a splendid opportunity, you know, for realizing our ambassadorship. It's very odd to reflect what a lot of the good marks some of us will get at our last account will be for keeping our tempers, just, with great difficulty, keeping our tempers, at moments when nobody imagined we were in any danger of losing them.

And then you have a list, I think, of four qualities which the perfect ambassador ought to have. St. Paul always pitches his standard high. I don't know how you are to translate that word *hagnotes*. "Chastity", yes; but the word has a merely negative sound. *Hagnotes* is a quality so pure as to be terrible; it dazzles you, no embattled array so awes men's hearts. A convoy passing through a country town, that endless stream of fortified motion, how it takes your breath away with the realization of the terrific thing modern war is! Something like that ought to be the purity of the priest. Not just the insensitiveness of the bachelor, who finds women a nuisance, not the furtive horror which tries to forget that sex exists, but something unapproachable, blinding, on a different plane from thoughts of evil. What a waste of God's gifts, when the life that is pledged to celibacy is not a life irradiated by purity! When brooding regrets, or cheap familiarities, tarnish the surface of that mirror which ought to reflect Christ!

"Knowledge"—how curiously St. Paul compiles his lists! Only this is not the kind of knowledge in which you can take doctorates. Always, I think, the idea in St. Paul's mind when he uses this word is that of familiarity with the things of the supernatural world, a familiarity which only comes from prayer. "He was in the world . . . and the world knew him not"—it is the opposite of that attitude which St. Paul means by knowledge; a recognition which has grown into familiarity. The soil on which an embassy is built belongs, by diplomatic usage, to the country which that embassy represents. And the ground on which the priest's feet tread should be, as it were, part of the soil of heaven transplanted to earth. The language of heaven should be talked in the presbytery, as the English language is talked in the British Embassy at Moscow. The layman who is in a difficulty ought to say to himself, "I'll go and talk to the priest about it, he'll be able to tell me; he knows God". The laity at large have the impression, and rightly, I think, that we priests know our job. I sometimes wonder whether they have the same confidence that we know our Employer.

"Long-suffering"—the difference between that and the patience we were speaking of just now leaps to the eye. You can be patient about things; an illness or a sleepless night; you are long-suffering only about persons. More, you are patient with people when they bore you or badger you without meaning any harm; you are long-suffering only where there is a sense of injury. And this quality, in one of Christ's ambassadors, is evidently of the first importance. We carry his ultimatum in our pockets; that puts us in a very delicate position. On the one hand, we have to portray him to the faithful as infinitely forgiving; we shall not do that if we are unforgiving people ourselves. On the other hand, it will sometimes be our duty to tell a fellow-mortal, "No, if you go on like that, if you persist in doing that, there is no forgiveness for you, in this world or in the world to come". Essential that the man who speaks like that should not be thought to be putting any personal animus into the declaration; the sinful soul must never be allowed to think "He is saying that because he has a down on me". And that is what people are very apt to say; cast your mind back to school days, and remember how when you were punished it was always because that professor had a down on you. The priest, then, must be known as one who *personally* harbours no grudges, who forgets an injury. When the sinner is told by such a man as that that there is no forgiveness, he will begin to take notice. Do let us beware of using phrases, even in fun, which will send round the parish the impression that we are unforgiving people.

"Sweetness" will not quite do in English, though *suavitas* might do in Latin, for *chrestotes*. *Chrestos* is a word St. Paul is fond of applying to Almighty God himself; "kindness" would do, but I think "graciousness" does better. Here you have the positive side of the picture; our Lord's ambassadors must represent him as being, not only forgiving to the sinner, but gracious to all his suppliants. And if we are to represent our Lord to the people in that light, we shall do it best by having a graciousness of our own which represents his. There is a kind of universal benevolence which sometimes makes itself felt, even in a very shy man, even in a very reserved man, which does win souls. Everybody calls the priest "dear old" Father So-and-so, if not actually "poor old" Father So-and-so; there are no organizations in the parish and the accounts are in a frightful mess, but somehow people go to church. It is *chrestotes* that has done it.

The pure-minded priest, the priest who is familiar with God, who is forgiving, who is gracious—having asked all that of us, St. Paul goes on to give us four resources we have to rely on, if we are going to face this tremendous task. The Holy Spirit; I wonder if we think enough about all that? I mean, we are apt, some of us, to be rather like the minister who said "If I'm called upon to speak suddenly like this, I just say what the Holy Spirit puts into my mind, but if you'll give me an hour or two for preparation, I can do much better". We get into the pulpit without any sermon prepared, because we have been prevented, by sick calls or some other unexpected interruption, from giving it the time we meant to. And no doubt the Holy Spirit does give us special assistance then, but isn't it giving him a rather secondary role if we *only* expect him to help us out on occasions like that? Surely we ought to pray to him more, try and make ourselves more supple to his influence, than we do. After all, most of us have known, in the confessional perhaps, what it is to say something which we aren't in the least expecting to say, can't quite make out afterwards why we did say it; isn't that perhaps meant to make us see that we have more help at hand than we mostly realize? Isn't it meant to make us trust, rather more, the occasional impulse we get to say something—only we're too shy; to write a letter to somebody—only we're too slack? Don't let us be neglectful in our devotion to the Holy Spirit; the ambassador has got to keep in touch with Headquarters.

Then there is unaffected love, love unfeigned. It may be the business of the ordinary ambassador to feign love; to pretend great friendliness towards the country in which he is stationed, when in fact he feels no such friendliness, and knows that his countrymen don't either. We are in a better position than that; we are bound to our congregations by a real tie of Christian fellowship, of pastoral good-will, which will triumph, if we will let it, over many difficulties.

And then "the word of truth": or as we should say, "the truth of our message". The ordinary ambassador is fairly often under an obligation—what shall we say? Sir William Temple observed that an ambassador is one who goes and lies abroad for his country. Let us say anyhow that he is often in a position where he has to let the foreign statesmen he is conversing with deceive themselves—about his own country's resources, his own country's intentions. The ambassador of Christ suffers from no such embarrassment as that; he is simply speaking the truth that is in his heart.

And finally, the power of God—we must not expect God to do miracles for us; but he has waiting for us, if we will trust him, unexpected providences; an important conversion, a big cheque, you never know what. So, when its ambassador is not being listened to, a country will sometimes reinforce his authority by making a demonstration, mobilizing its troops, or something of that sort. Heaven does back up its ambassadors.

At this point St. Paul, whose thought plays about like lightning, disconcerts us a little by apparently beginning to say the exact opposite of what he has been saying before. He has been telling us how important it is that the ambassadors of Christ should make a good impression, and then quite suddenly he adds: "After all, what does it matter what people think of us? Makes no difference at all". The reason is, I think, that (as you will find at the beginning of the letter) people at Corinth have been saying nasty things about St. Paul. They said he was a man you couldn't trust, and he didn't like that. But he reminds himself now that what people think of us doesn't in the least matter. Well, it isn't really the opposite of what has gone before. I think if he had expressed himself rather more coherently, he would have said, "It is the business of Christ's ambassador to make the most favourable impression he can. Having done that, he must not be in the least surprised if in spite of it people think ill of him; they always will". And we, while (as I've been trying to point out) we have an urgent duty to make people think well of us, must be quite unmoved, in ourselves, by their approval or disapproval. It all means nothing.

We are to be armed on the right as well as on the left; your ancient soldier carried his shield on his left arm, and fought that side first. But it isn't really satisfactory only to have a pad on the leg that is facing the bowling. No, we must be armed right and left with justice, by which I think St. Paul here means innocence. It doesn't very much matter, because he has got his metaphor mixed up; what he is trying to say is that we should be equally steeled against undue blame and undue praise. "By honour and dishonour, by evil report and good report". The best-looking girl in the parish goes and marries a Protestant, when you've moved heaven and earth to prevent it; and then you hear the Protestants are saying that you deliberately threw her in the poor boy's way, so as to try and pervert him. Don't mind; it won't do any harm. On the other hand, don't be too ready to believe all the good you hear about yourself. The intense woman who says, "Father, that marvellous sermon of yours"; the enthusiastic parishioner who says, "Ah, sure, Almighty God sent us a good priest when he sent you, Father"—write it off; that kind of thing won't save you any Purgatory.

Then the rest of the epistle merely carries a list of the unkind things people say about God's ambassadors; the instances chosen are very much of St. Paul's own day, and I fancy very much concerned with St. Paul's own experience. He had critics at Corinth, and they had been saying that he was a liar; that he was unacknowledged (that is, the other apostles didn't recognize him as an apostle); that it didn't matter what his teaching was, because he was probably dead in any case; or if not dead, so badly mauled by the mob at Ephesus that he would be no use again; that he was always writing tearful letters, and making people feel uncomfortable; that he was always begging for money; that he had no rich friends, and couldn't expect to make a success of preaching the gospel.

All that we probably shan't hear about ourselves. But we shall hear very much that sort of thing said about the Church we love more than life. That our claims are built on false-hood; that we are an insignificant force in the world to-day; that we are dying out, or at least have lost so much prestige that we shall never recover from it; that we are kill-joys, preaching a medieval morality to a world which has grown out of it; that we are always on the make, always in alliance with the rich against the poor, with the Have's against the Have-not's; or, contrary-wise, that we are a very provincial, middle-class set of people, we Catholics, what we do isn't worth reporting, what we say isn't worth repeating. All that we shall hear said, or read it in books and newspaper articles by people who don't like us. But none of it matters; none of it matters a bit, as long as we haven't been responsible, for giving a bad impression of the ministry we exercise; as long as we, Christ's ambassadors, have done our best to do what nobody can ever really do—represent him.

# 4

# SINS OF THE PRIEST

There are few more splendidly menacing
phrases in the whole of Hebrew prophecy than the words
with which Amos, the first prophet whose message has come
down to us in writing, turns suddenly on the people of Israel
in one of its rare intervals of prosperity. He has announced
God's impending judgements on certain neighbouring tribes,
on Syria, Ammon, Moab, and so on; and then, turning to
the Israelites, he represents God as saying, "You only have
I known of all the families of the earth; therefore I will visit
upon you all your iniquities".

It is difficult to imagine anything which could have come
as more of a shock to the complacent theologians of his day.
Israel was God's chosen people, brought out of Egypt, led
through the desert, enabled to dispossess seven nations in
Chanaan and occupy their fertile territory. Was it not clear
that a people so signally favoured would continue to enjoy
his protection? True, there were backslidings and scandals;
the Israelites would adopt the worship of some heathen god

side by side with their own inherited traditions; there would be oppression of the poor, there would be grasping covetousness or open debauchery among the priests, and so on. But who could doubt, that if for a short while God's protection was forfeited by these infidelities, it would be restored to his people for the asking, after a decent show of contrition and amendment? As God's favourites, his people could afford to take liberties with him, to treat him as an indulgent Father; it was not likely that he would be hard on *them* considering all the promises which committed him to maintain their cause among the peoples. Them only God had known among all the families of the earth; surely he would be tolerant towards their occasional lapses!

To which Amos replies, in words of thunder, "You only have I known among all the families of the earth, THERE-FORE will I visit upon you all your iniquities". Because they had been given more chances; because a law had been issued to them on mount Sinai purer than any other code the world knew; because a long line of patriots and reformers had been sent to recall them, when they needed it, to a sense of religion, THEREFORE the sins they committed were the less excusable, therefore their punishment would be all the more certain, and all the heavier.

I suppose there is always a danger that we Catholics shall be guilty of the same miscalculation. Looking round us on a world which seems to have lost, in such great part, its grasp of moral principle, a world in which we may read in our newspaper how some spokesman of religion has been calling the attention of our fellow-countrymen to the very existence of the Ten Commandments, we are tempted sometimes to a vague feeling of self-congratulation—after all, *somebody's* got to go to heaven. But what I want to suggest at the moment is that we priests run special risks of our own in this matter. Ordination has made us, in a special way, friends of Jesus Christ; we are always in and out of church, always running God's errands; he commissions us to speak in his name; our very faults arise so much out of the nature of the work we do for him, through being in a hurry, through being tired, through being lonely; all our life is so bound up with religion, it is all such a family affair—surely, unless we go very far wrong, he will not let *us* down? But I fancy if the prophet Amos heard us thinking like that, he would say to us too, "You only have I known of all the families of the earth, therefore will I visit upon you all your iniquities".

Always, I think, though in different ways, the fact of being a priest increases the malice of our sin. If we were really honest with ourselves, I'm not sure we shouldn't tack that on to all the items of our confessions; "I've been proud, and I'm a priest. I've been grasping with money, and I'm a priest. I have offended against modesty, and I'm a priest. I have lost my temper, and I'm a priest. I've been self-indulgent, and I'm a priest. I have envied others, and I'm a priest. I've been idle; I, a priest, have been idle. And all the other sins, which I cannot now remember, are the sins of a priest".

May we just go through them, in an old-fashioned way, those seven capital sins, fountain-heads of our sinning, ingredients which form the basis of all those subtle flavours which our sins bring with them?

Pride first; pride will come first, even on such a list as this. Pride, in its pure form, is seldom recognizable; but when it appears as ambition, as vanity, as obstinacy, as touchiness, as self-sufficiency, as the love of interference, it is common enough; not unknown among priests. You find So-and-so a bore; look into your heart, and ask whether it was not because he held the floor when you wanted to be talking. Your advice is not asked, or is taken and not followed; you sulk. You are asked to undertake some job; you excuse yourself— nominally from humility, because you say you are no good at that sort of thing, really because you can't bear the thought of doing something badly, and looking a fool. In all that, you are coming short of the priestly character. For the priesthood dates from the last Supper; and the charter of its foundation is, "He that is greatest among you all, let him be the servant of all; I am among you as he that serveth". When those words were spoken, a servant meant a slave. To-day, slavery has been abolished, and at the moment even domestic service seems to be becoming a thing of the past. But always it will be the priest's primary duty to serve; and a fault in humility cuts at the very roots of the priestly character. It identifies you with the attitude of that first rebel who said, *Non serviam.*

Avarice, of all the capital sins, can be the most tragic, because it does not die down with old age; sometimes old age brings it on. Personal avarice is rare in priests, just because we are not in much of a position either to indulge it, or to benefit by it. But it is possible for a man to become avaricious when he is administering, quite conscientiously, funds committed to his charge; and the delicate position in which our mission funds stand, having to provide for the maintenance of the clergy as well as the maintenance of the parish, gives a kind of edge to the eagerness with which the acquisitive rector hunts pennies. Sometimes, too, with the feeling that a good object justifies shady methods—a doctrine which we do not preach, and have to spend a large part of our time explaining to Protestants that we do not preach it; sometimes, with that idea vaguely in mind, a priest will be guilty of graft or evasion which he would scorn to indulge in, if it were for the sake of his own pocket. But avarice is avarice still, and graft is graft and evasion is evasion still, however laudable the object for which we are working.

And this sin is especially to be blamed in the clergy, for two reasons. In the first place, there is nothing like avarice for shutting up the sympathies of the human heart. The man who is always thinking about money, whether in connexion with football pools or in connexion with the new sacristy, cannot have his heart open, as the priest should, to the troubles, the anxieties, the interests of others. And in the second place, nothing gives so much scandal, of a suppressed kind, as the perpetual suspicion that the clergy are on the make. One of the chief causes which has long held up, and still holds up, the conversion of England, is the fact that Protestants cannot go to our churches without submitting to a long harangue about money, in the notices, in the sermon, or in both, which nearly always takes the form of a scolding. Adrian Fortescue used to say it was a Providence that Protestants always accuse us of charging five shillings for hearing confessions, because as a matter of fact absolution was the one thing you could get for nothing in the Catholic Church. There is, at the moment, a distrust of organized religion such as has never existed in England be-

fore. Can we do nothing to dispel it, by keeping that clank-
ing money-box out of sight?

Of sins against modesty I don't want to say much. God
gives us this grace in dealing with them, that it is in our
nature to be ashamed of them. It needs no proof that a
priest who sins against modesty in such a way as to involve
the least breath of scandal, is false to his priesthood. Every
priest is a Joseph, set by our Lord over his household with a
special view to watching over its purity; a sheep-dog which
starts running sheep is less unprofitable to its master, than a
scandal-giving priest is to his. That, I hope, is clear enough
to all of us. But even the secret sins of a priest have a special
danger for him. The effect of self-indulgence which sins
against modesty is, we are told, to turn a man in upon himself, make him self-centred and selfish. Let us remind ourselves again that no priest can afford to encourage in himself
that fatal tendency we all have to selfishness. Merely to get
through our work, as work, without taking a vivid interest
in the people we are working for—how terribly common that
is, and how grievously it retards the reign of Christ!

And now, what shall we say about anger? May I say, quite
bluntly, that we priests in England are apt, I think, to be too
brusque, too hectoring, in our dealings with the faithful;
there is too much of the drill-sergeant about us? Scolding
in the confessional, I suppose, means six souls lost for one
saved. But I am thinking more of our daily contacts. I admit
that the laity don't always make it easy for us. A lot of mis-
understanding would be saved if they would realize that the
best time for buttonholing a priest and having a cosy chat is
not just before he says his second Mass on a busy Sunday.

But those little outbursts of temper, even with the altar-boys, even with the beggars, what a lot of harm they can do! I wonder how much of the leakage we often hear talked about is due to the plain fact that the people are afraid of their clergy? The sons of Heli "withdrew men from the sacrifice of the Lord"; what more terrible epitaph could there be on a priest than that?

Let me be still more bold, and say that I think the worst possible scene of clerical ill-temper is the pulpit. It's a very easy way of sounding rather effective in your sermons; there are grievances you have been nursing all the week—perhaps it is the stinginess of your congregation, or some members of it; perhaps it is a piece of parish gossip that has come to your ears, and made you genuinely indignant. You go up into the pulpit with nothing prepared, and all your grievances come out with a rush and a roar. There may be some Protestant husband who has been persuaded by his wife, with infinite difficulty, to come to Mass just this once, and see what it's like—he comes just this once, and he knows what it's like after that. There may be some bad Catholic, already half-lapsed, looking about for an excuse to call the Church hard names; what wonder, if after all that torrent of abuse he goes home declaring that he has finished with it now? The sacristan is delighted with you; when you get back to the sacristy, he says, "My word, Father, you gave it them straight this morning". I think it is a good rule, if the sacristan says "My word, Father, you gave it them straight this morning", to tear up the notes of that sermon at once, if there were any, and to ask God on your knees that he will never let you preach a sermon like that again.

I don't want to talk much about gluttony. I don't even want to improve the occasion by talking about the dangers of drinking to excess; unless for the benefit of the younger fathers present I may be allowed to repeat to you the advice I always gave to undergraduates when they were going to attend public dinners; "Wait till you find yourself saying, Just this glass can't do me any harm, and then, don't drink it". But I thought I would like to say a word about self-indulgence generally on the part of the clergy as that affects the question of scandal, and more than ever in these times. We have lived so far in an England which tolerated class distinctions; tolerated, therefore, sharp and obvious differences of income. The Catholic clergy did not fit into any particular class; it was right that they should not. Consequently, it was nobody's business to enquire whether the Catholic clergy did themselves well or not. I don't personally believe that England will soon have abolished class distinctions, or will soon have abolished sharp differences of income. But I do think there will be a lot of talk about these things, and there will be a large, discontented part of the population which will look round jealously to see who is rich, and to wonder why. In such a state of society, it will be a bad thing for the Catholic cause if our clergy seem to be doing themselves too well; if their cars look too new and they appear to be throwing their weight about when they go off for their summer holiday. Because the clergy are a separate caste, it is easier for people to generalize about their habits. And the sin of self-indulgence will be all the worse in the clergy, because it will bring the Church into disrepute.

The sin of envy (or, if we may use the wider term, of

jealousy) is one which has devastating effects; effects, primarily, on the character of the man who is addicted to it, and on his conversation. May I shelter myself behind my own advancing years, and say that I think we older priests are the worst offenders? For this reason, I suppose, chiefly—that a man seldom reaches the age of fifty without beginning to feel a bit of a failure. And we take it out of our neighbours by crabbing their performances. So-and-so, who couldn't hold a candle to us at college, has gone ahead and become an important person; and we find it necessary to be catty about that. The religious next door get big congregations, make a lot of converts—but then, look at the way they go about it! And all the rest of it; I'm afraid our conversation isn't very enlivening, when the grievances begin to be trotted out. All the time, you see, we are really trying to apply balm to our injured self-esteem. I always liked the story of the American school-master who was hauling one of his pupils over the coals for idleness, and said he supposed the boy had a pretty considerable veneration for the name of George Washington. And when the boy allowed he had, the school-master said, "Then let me tell you that when he was your age, George Washington was head of his class." And the boy replied, "Yes, Sir, and when he was your age he was President of the United States." No, we're not Presidents of the United States; there are youthful ambitions that lie behind us, unfulfilled. Are we much to blame, if we sometimes attack what seem to us shallow reputations?

Let us be clear, at least, about this—the rector of a parish is responsible in God's sight, not only for his parish, but for his curates. The disgruntled, disillusioned rector can be a blight on young lives, can throw a cold douche on young ambitions, as no one else can, and the results may be appalling. "Try it if you like, my dear father, but you'll find you get no response from the people, absolutely none; I've lived in this parish twenty years, and I know them." How often that is the encouragement the young curate gets, when he is rash enough to propose trying experiments! And tell me, how much of that is due to the fear that another might succeed where you have failed? Oh, the terrible dead-weight of that elderly conservatism which is jealous of young men, because they are young; jealous on behalf of old methods, not because they succeeded, but because they were our methods, and no others must be allowed to succeed!

The last place on the list has a curious history. The medievals gave it to Accidie, a word which has gone out of use, and perhaps can be most succinctly defined as getting bored with religion. That is a very real danger; I only don't consider it here, because I want to devote a whole meditation to it later on. To-day, we have substituted the word "sloth"; a failing from which we all suffer, and one which none of us ever admits. I think the best way of examining your conscience, if you want to discover whether you are an idle man, is to leave on one side all the things which interest you—and that, naturally, includes a great deal of your parish work—and concentrate on some side-line of your daily habits which doesn't interest you; say, writing letters. Are you an energetic correspondent? The clergy very seldom are. Or that book, a bit on the heavy side, which you bought the other day, meaning to read it; how many of the pages are cut? Idleness, with most of us, doesn't mean lying in bed and doing nothing; it means giving priority, always, to the things which interest us, and leaving our other duties to queue up and take their turn, if they ever get a turn. Watch idleness; it can become a sort of creeping paralysis, which can infect even your priestly duties in the end. And an idle parish priest puts out a light in God's Church.

He has not called us his servants, but his friends. That should be our inspiration; that, also, should be our warning; shall he be in a position to say to us, "It was thou, my own familiar friend, in whom I trusted"? If so, what wonder that he should add, "You only have I known among all the families of the earth, THEREFORE will I visit upon you all your iniquities"?

# 5

# ST. PAUL, A PROFILE

I want to give you a profile of St. Paul as a human being, the raw material which was towed into Damascus after that road accident; not so much a panegyric as a portrait from the life. There are various reasons, I think, why we should content ourselves with that treatment. Partly because the moment you begin preaching a panegyric, every saint becomes very much like any other saint. Partly because St. Paul had, I think, a great deal of character; there was more in his *naturel*, if I may borrow a word from the French for which we have no word in English, than in that of many of the saints. I mean, I think he would have been a remarkable and an interesting man even if he had not been a saint, just as St. Francis of Sales and Dom Bosco, for instance, would have been remarkable and interesting men even if they had not been saints. Partly because the evidence is so full; I doubt if there is any other human being, before St. Francis of Assisi, anyhow, for whom we have so much material for constructing a biography; Cicero is the only person who can at all challenge him there, and Cicero to tell the truth was rather a dull person, which St. Paul was not. We have all these very intimate letters of his, we have a careful account of a considerable period of his life written by a great friend and disciple of his, who knew how to write. So let us try and get underneath the halo and see St. Paul as a living person. I think it will be possible, as we go along, to pick up one or two hints about our own priestly lives; about the right way to tackle ourselves and other people.

First of all, I think it is obvious that St. Paul had a quick nature; he was the sort of person who speaks first and thinks afterwards. Our Lord seems to have chosen people of that kind for the pioneer work of his Church; St. Peter obviously was one, and I think St. Stephen was another. He didn't choose only that kind of person; St. James, I should say, was very much the opposite, a man of caution—listen to him telling the other apostles the Gentiles ought certainly to be given the greatest possible freedom, always as long as they don't eat things which have been strangled. St. Paul was not that kind of man; he was the sort of man who rushed at things. Watch him at Athens; he has not gone there to preach, he is simply waiting till his friends join him, then he will go on to Corinth. But he cannot bear the sight of all these people pretending to be philosophers and at the same time worshipping gods of wood and stone; his heart was moved within him to find the city so much given over to idolatry; he stops everyone he meets and argues about it.

And because St. Paul's was an impulsive temperament, he says what he thinks, sometimes, with startling vividness. When he is writing to the Galatian Christians, for example, about the people who want to have them all circumcised; "I would rather they should lose their own manhood, these authors of your unrest". That is the kind of sentence which your modern editor of a saint's life would be apt to leave out; and write in a bit more about the spirit of patience which the holy man displayed towards his enemies. Of course, I have no doubt at all that it was justifiable moral indignation; but I refuse to believe St. Paul did not throw himself into it. All through the Galatians, he is writing at white heat, and you can see that he is riding himself on the curb; it's a wonderful specimen of a letter from an angry man which just manages to avoid being an angry letter.

And then, there is another side to the picture; this impulsive temperament, which makes St. Paul so indignant when a wrong is being done to the cause of Christ, makes him infinitely tender as soon as repentance is shewn. You find that, for example, in his second epistle to the Corinthians. He had written them a letter—I think it is generally agreed that it was not our First Corinthians, but a letter now lost—in which he called upon them to administer discipline to an offender, probably someone who had slighted his own authority. No sooner does he hear this has been done, than he writes off to them in a very different tone. "Even if I caused you pain by my letter, I am not sorry for it. Perhaps I was tempted to be sorry when I saw how my letter had caused you even momentary pain, but now I am glad, not glad of the pain, but glad of the repentance the pain brought with it . . . You have done everything to prove yourselves free from guilt in this matter . . . The punishment inflicted on him by so many of you is punishment enough for the man I speak of, and now you must rather think of shewing him indulgence, and comforting him." St. Paul is almost embarrassed by the success of his own tactics; he never really expected the opposition to crumple up as it has.

Some of us are impulsive by nature, and inclined by nature to go off the deep end. Having a row with the parish, or a section of the parish, is sometimes necessary. There has been a row, perhaps unnecessarily precipitated by my shortness of temper, but anyhow, it seems to have done good; the parish has rallied round properly, and the air has cleared. Now is the time for me to score a double success, by taking my victory in the right way. Not crowing over it, not throwing my weight about; not (above all) victimizing any particular person or persons who are thought to have been at the root of the trouble. No, just the opposite; soothing injured feelings wherever I can by a deliberate effort of friendliness. And when you want to shew a person friendliness, the best way is often asking him to do something for you.

Meanwhile, let us notice one thing about St. Paul when he was having a row, or indeed whenever he was trying to get his own way—that is, Christ's way. He always preferred to lead from weakness, rather than from strength. There's very little doubt, I think, that when he speaks of "the power" which is given him as an apostle he means miraculous power, such as he exercised when he punished the magician Elymas with sudden blindness. And there is always this threat in the background; when the apostle comes on his next visit, he will know how to deal with people who obstinately oppose him. But before that happens, he is always desperately anx-

ious to win as many people as possible to a better mind by
appealing, not to his power, but to his weakness.

That is the meaning of all that long epistle about St.
Paul's hardships and persecutions. He hated talking about
himself; he always prefers the word "We" to the word "I";
but on an occasion like this he deliberately went all out to
make the Corinthians feel sorry for him, so as to bring them
up to time by sympathy, rather than by fear. And in a quite
different connexion, when he writes to Philemon asking him
to be kind to his runaway slave Onesimus, he could have
taken a high line about it; Philemon was his own convert,
perhaps literally owed his life to St. Paul, but that is not the
appeal that shall be put in the forefront. "Who is it that
writes to thee? Paul, an old man now, and in these days the
prisoner, too, of Jesus Christ." I don't think that St. Paul
liked appealing for sympathy any more than most of us do.
But he saw that if that motive would induce his converts
to do the right thing, it was a good kind of motive for them
to have; better than the fear of being struck blind on St.
Paul's next visit.

Well, we are not in a position to strike our parishioners
blind when they disagree with us. We priests in our parishes
are not even in a position to threaten them with any severe
spiritual penalties, beyond being turned out of the choir, or
something of that kind. But we have a sort of undefined
ascendancy in the parish, which is quite unlike anything
that is enjoyed by the Anglican Vicar over the way; very
few people, in a healthy parish, like to be on bad terms with
the parish priest. And we are a little tempted, I think, to
trade on that fact; to crush opposition by a hint that any-

body who sees differently from the parish priest must be rather a rotten sort of Catholic. That line—or perhaps "line" is too definite a word; that sort of approach—is responsible, I am afraid, for a good many tragedies. That boy who has only just left school, so that we still think of him as a kind of fag, is earning four pounds a week now, and eager to assert his independence. I wonder whether sometimes, when we want to put a stop to what seems undesirable, or to have something done for us, we couldn't afford to take the line, rather more, of saying "Look here, I'm in a bit of a hole, I wonder whether you could help to get me out of it?" That, I think, is what St. Paul would like us to say. I think it went against the grain with him, but he did it.

In those ways, I think we are tempted to treat our parishioners rather too much as children. Meanwhile, do we really treat them as our children? St. Paul has an almost frightening phrase, you will remember, about that; "My little children; with whom I am in travail again until Christ be formed in you". It's a mixed metaphor, of course; St. Paul was never afraid of mixing his metaphors. He thinks of himself, both as the mother who has borne these children to Christ, and as the midwife who must see Christ born in them. But what a terrible responsibility it indicates! Each soul in my parish a soul in which Christ is to be born, and it is my job to see that that happens! It was said to me long ago, by an old priest, "I've been in this parish thirty years, and I've always paid my way". I don't quite know why I mention that; let it be enough to observe that I can't imagine St. Paul saying it. My little children, helpless, unformed as yet; capable of developing so far in the right direction or the wrong direction; and the responsibility, a great share of the responsibility, lies with me. And not just in a crowd, so as to make me responsible for the general tone of the parish, but each one individually. I am ready enough to call them "my child" in the confessional, with a slight emphasis on the word "child"; have I always thought of the emphasis there ought to be on the word "my"?

That is worth remembering, if I ever find myself wondering whether I don't shew too much preference for the society of this or that person, this or that family, in my congregation. I am not talking now of intimacies that might bring danger with them, or even intimacies that might bring scandal with them; but we all have our favourites; it would be hardly human nature if we didn't. And I think there were certain people whose company was a real refreshment to St. Paul, one of the few refreshments he ever allowed himself in his busy, concentrated life. "There is one who never fails to comfort those who are brought low; God gave us comfort, as soon as Titus came." "I shall be sending Timothy to visit you before long; . . . I have no one else here who shares my thoughts as he does." "Greetings from my beloved Luke, the physician." Oh yes, St. Paul had his special friends. What did he do about it?

I think his advice to us would have been, "By all means have your special friends; only, be sure of one thing—be sure that everybody else in the parish is your special friend as well". That, I think, is the moral of the sixteenth chapter of the Romans. St. Paul had never been to Rome; yet he fills his sixteenth chapter with two dozen personal salutations, to the despair of the refectory reader. They had been refugees, presumably, at the time when Claudius published his edict banishing the Jews from Rome, and St. Paul had met them in the Levant. They did not suppose, I take it, that they had made any special impression on the great missionary; how suddenly splendid to hear their own names mentioned when the letter was read out, as I expect it was, in the Roman Church! One or two of them were marked out by terms of endearment, "Amplias whom I love so well in the Lord, my dear Stachys, my dear Persis". But what did that matter to the rest of them, so long as they were all there, Asyncritus, Phlegon, Hermas, and all the others?

Let me not ask myself, "Do I see too much of So-and-so? Do I spend too much of my time with this particular family?" But ask rather, for a change, "Do I see enough of all the other people who aren't So-and-so? Do I spend enough of my time with other families, who don't amuse me quite as much as this one?" I think it is nonsense to pretend that for most of us it is possible to work fruitfully for the souls of our fellow-creatures without establishing human contacts all the time. Yet it is very easy for a priest who is not a good mixer to imagine that it is rather holy of him to pass his life without saying a word except to his fellow-clergy. In such a lot of our work we are, and are meant to be, holy machines, that it is easy to forget the duty of being anything else. You go out after breakfast to give some Sick Communions, and naturally you have your eyes on the ground, take no notice of anyone who passes you. Then, in the afternoon, you go out for a walk; there may be a temptation to go about even then looking as if you were saying your prayers, merely out of shyness, or merely because you are afraid of meeting bores. But what a difference it makes, when one goes out for a walk with some parish priest, and finds that he has to lift his hat to every second person he meets, stop and talk to every fifth or sixth! What a lot of good they do without knowing it, those priests! What a lot of harm can be done, sometimes, by a salute unreturned!

I mentioned just now my old friend who had paid his way for thirty years, and perhaps seemed to contrast his point of view with St. Paul's. But not, heaven knows, that St. Paul was not interested in the collections. There never was such a beggar as St. Paul. I suppose if you analysed his epistles you would find that about one chapter in four is really talking about the Jerusalem distress fund. The reason why one doesn't notice it more is because St. Paul was a shy sort of beggar, an elusive sort of beggar. Look at the innocent way in which he tells the Romans that he may be having to go to Jerusalem to bring alms there: "Macedonia and Achaia have thought fit to give those saints in Jerusalem who are in need some share of their wealth . . . and indeed, they are in their debt. The Gentiles, if they have been allowed to share their spiritual gifts, are bound to contribute to their temporal needs in return". Wasn't he trying to make the Romans think a bit? But even when he is openly begging, how gently he insinuates his point; how tactfully he makes the Corinthians see that if they aren't careful Macedonia will head the list of subscribers, not Achaia!

Perhaps there is a sort of a tail-end of a lesson for some of us there. We are not all of us shy and elusive, when we get into the pulpit, about this particular subject. You hear, not seldom, of lay people who don't go to such and such a church because it's money, money, money week after week in the sermons there. St. Paul managed to wrap it up, somehow, better than we do. And also, he was very careful indeed not to give scandal by sounding for a moment as if he personally was interested in the result of the appeal. He would slave at tent-making rather than even have Pharisaical scandal going round about his motives. It is our privilege to live of the gospel; we must perhaps be a little extra careful, in these days, not to look too much as if we made a good thing out of it.

One other point; for all his quick temperament, St. Paul was splendidly free from jealousy. When he writes from his Roman prison to Philippi, he explains how other Christians at Rome, who don't approve of him, have started preaching the gospel all the harder, so as not to be outbidden. "What matter, so long as either way, for private ends or in all honesty, CHRIST is preached?" So it is everywhere; what does it matter whether Paul or Apollo is the apostle of Corinth? I planted, and Apollo watered, but it is God who gives the increase. Shall we remember, sometimes, those splendid words used by a rather sensitive man, a rather touchy man, about the very rivals who were being cried up as his superiors? Remember them, when the queue at somebody else's confessional is a bit longer than the queue at ours; when somebody else's sermons seem to draw a better congregation than ours?

I have only just begun talking about St. Paul. I promised a profile of him, and I've only given the skimpiest possible kind of vignette. But we can fill out the picture for ourselves well enough by reading between the lines of his epistles.

"Be followers of me", he is not ashamed to say, "as I am of Christ". Do we find it difficult, sometimes, to make out what our Lord would have done if he had been faced with such and such problems of ours? Let us see if we cannot find out what St. Paul would have done, and do that; we shall not go very far wrong.

# 6

## MURMURING

There is a famous passage in his first epistle to the Corinthians, where St. Paul warns them against some of their leading faults, and reminds them that the same faults were found, and were severely punished, among the Israelites in the wilderness. Idolatry, for he is writing to a church of recent converts; fornication, since Corinth was notorious even in a generally corrupt age, for the looseness of its morals; "tempting God", that is to say, presuming on grace, because evidently there was a tendency abroad, a Calvinistic tendency you might say, which was exposing his converts to great spiritual dangers. And he adds a fourth warning, against murmuring. I think the point of that was, that there were factions at Corinth, parties which took their slogans from this leader or that; and it reminded St. Paul of those ill-fated revolutionaries who questioned, in the wilderness, the divinely-appointed authority of Moses. "Neither be ye murmurers, as some of them murmured, and were destroyed by the destroyer."

The children of Israel murmured—what a familiar phrase that is, to anybody who knows his Old Testament! I shouldn't like to say how many times it occurs in the Mosaic writings. And at first sight it seems a very extraordinary thing, doesn't it? Here is a people to which God has shewed special favour, visiting their oppressors in Egypt with ten plagues from which they themselves were immune; then delivering them from Egypt by a miracle, dividing the Red Sea for them and bringing the waters together again to drown their pursuers; leading them through the desert, watching over them, giving them bread from heaven and water out of the rock, promising them an end to their journey in a land that flowed with milk and honey. And those are the people who seem to spend the greater part of their forty years in the wilderness murmuring against God, or against the rulers he has set up over them. It seems extraordinary, doesn't it? And yet . . . I wonder.

Could God have done more than he does for us Christians, for us priests? He has called us out of the world to serve him; he feeds us with the bread of immortality; he opens to us the consolations of his Sacred Heart; and all that is not enough to keep us from complaining, some of us complaining almost continually, of the lines in which our lot is cast. Nor are we content to bear a grudge against life in general; commonly at least we put the blame on our fellow-men; on superiors who seem unsympathetic, on colleagues who are uncongenial, on parishioners who are difficult. Will you forgive me, Reverend Fathers, if I devote a whole meditation to this uncharitable habit of grumbling, which does so much to mar the perfect offering of our lives to God?

After all, you have got to remember, in excuse for the Israelites, that Moses did lead them out into a wilderness. Sometimes, if their march did not proceed according to schedule, their water supply was insufficient; their food, however plentiful, had some of that monotony which belongs to picnic fare. It was only natural for them to remember that in Egypt, for all their servitude, they had no difficulty in providing themselves with creature comforts: "We remember the fish that we ate in Egypt, and the leeks, and the cucumbers, and the melons"—fish and leeks and cucumbers and melons; watery sort of food, not much in the way of vitamins there. And yet it is possible to look back with regret to such delicacies when you are getting nothing to eat but manna and quails year in, year out. The life of the wilderness is a life of freedom, but the freedom is won at the cost of self-denial. And when you enter a seminary or a religious house, you are entering a life of freedom, in a sense; you are emancipating yourself from the clogging ties of worldly preoccupation. But in the outward scheme and structure of your life there must be a certain constraint. Rules cramp you; the average man is catered for, not the exception. It is not easy to live contentedly in a wilderness, or in a community.

And there is another point to be remembered—going out into the wilderness and shutting ourselves off from the world does bring us perilously close together. While they were still in Egypt, the Israelites probably spent a large part of their time murmuring against their task-masters, and no great harm was done. While they were living in a strange land, their race-consciousness, still so remarkable in our own day, fostered a spirit of loyalty among themselves. When they got out into the desert and there were no task-masters to murmur against, when they enjoyed no society except their own, they very quickly began to find out each other's weak points. So we, as long as we are living in the world, brushing up against a lot of strangers every day, moving in a lot of circles which do not intersect, find little temptation to spend our time in gossiping. But, once shut up a set of human beings within four walls, and, heavens, how the tongues begin to wag! No, living among your fellow-priests may safeguard you from every other kind of sin; it is not going to safeguard you against sins of the tongue unless you have a rule of perpetual silence.

Perhaps you will complain that I am really trying to treat two different failings of our nature as one; our tendency to grumble about the circumstances of life, and our tendency to criticize one another in an uncharitable way. Well, it's quite true that they are two different manifestations of an ungenerous temper; but I think it's also true that they are two manifestations of the same ungenerous temper. Your grumbler, as a rule, is also the man who can be trusted to pull a friend's character to pieces. And there's a further point; I think the grumbling I have in mind has usually a kind of personal tang about it; it is grumbling not merely about things, but about people. There is a tendency to identify, in a vague way, the faults you find in the system with the personalities of those who exercise authority over you. "The children of Israel murmured against Moses and Aaron"—not that Moses and Aaron were exempt from the privations which were felt by all; manna and quails figured as prominently in their diet as in anybody else's. But in order to voice a grievance properly you must have names to connect it with; Moses and Aaron had let them out into a wilderness, therefore they must be held responsible for any lack of amenities which the wilderness presented. I am speaking in parables, as St. Paul was; I don't know whether these parables will come home to you; they would have come home to us in the seminary from which my experience is drawn.

Now, I hope I shall not be understood as implying that there is no difference between criticizing your equals and criticizing your superiors. There is a different principle involved. But I want to consider the subject of murmuring generally; that is, of criticizing your neighbours, whether they are your superiors or your equals, merely by way of letting off steam; by way of indemnifying yourself for the discomforts of every-day life. As I say, it is a very difficult sin to avoid, when you are living in community, whether it be a large or a small community. But I do want to put it to you, for fear I might come short of my duty in giving this retreat, that murmuring is a nine-fold sin. It is a three-fold sin against God, a three-fold sin against your neighbour, and a three-fold sin against yourself.

Murmuring is a sin against God because it betrays a want of gratitude. After all, when you take a general view all round you, how pleasant other people are! How confiding they are, how good-natured, how considerate! How easily they win our sympathy, the moment we see them in a human light! Somebody who always got on your nerves, somebody you were always inclined to laugh at, suddenly has a bad accident, or suffers a family bereavement; and at once you begin to remember his good points, to make excuses for his failings—is that insincerity on your part? Why, no; but until he was in trouble you never really saw him as he was, never thought of him as your fellow-man. If only we were more simple, if only we didn't take things for granted so, we should see the whole of mankind, I think, as a gigantic conspiracy of kindness set on foot by Almighty God for our advantage; we should be overwhelmed with gratitude for the good offices done to us, with admiration at the fine qualities we see around us. Instead of which, we are always picking holes.

Murmuring is a sin against God because it betrays a want of confidence. When we criticize anybody, I am sure you must have noticed, it is not because we bear him any kind of ill-will, oh dear no, our personal feelings don't enter into the matter at all. No, we only mention it because it does seem a pity that a person like that should be in a position like that, with such possibilities for doing harm. It is wonderful how hot we grow in our altruistic indignation on such occasions as this; we feel the Church is being let down by being so unworthily represented in such and such a parish, in such and such a post of importance—that's what we mind. I say that this betrays a want of confidence in God. It was the spirit of the Israelites, when they asked Aaron to make a golden calf for them; "Arise, make us gods, that may go before us; for as for this Moses, we know not what is become of him". It's all very well, but what can you do with a man like that, who goes up to the top of a mountain, and leaves no word when he is to be expected back? . . . You know, it's the want of trust in God that makes us worry so much about the defects of his human agents. Believe me, if the Catholic Church had depended on human prudence for her survival, she would have gone into liquidation centuries ago. Every enterprise we undertake is in God's hands; those who direct its fortunes, do so under his overruling influence; to be so anxious about their qualifications is a poor kind of homage to him.

Murmuring is a sin against God because it betrays a want of detachment. There are very few of God's gifts which we use so lavishly, with so little regard to mortification, as the gift of speech. So much unnecessary talk; we surely ought to start cutting it down somewhere; and if we are going to have a cut somewhere, what more obvious place to begin at than our uncharitable conversations? Yet we don't seem to do it. How odd and how humiliating, that the one self-indulgence we find it impossible to deny ourselves should be this clatter-clatter of tongues over the shortcomings of other people!

And besides all this, in murmuring you are apt to inflict a three-fold injury on your neighbour. You injure the person you are talking about, the person you are talking to, and the person you are talking in front of. The person you are talking about, even if what you are saying is quite true, and even if the accusation is really quite a slight one, so that it does not take away his character. You are still belittling his stature in your own eyes and in the eyes of others by putting your thoughts about him into words. How often it happens that by summing up a person's character in an epigram, or finding a nickname to suit some oddity about him, you manage to pillory and perpetuate the memory of his shortcomings! And is there any gift God gives us which ought to be used with more earnest discretion than the gift of mimicry? You injure the person you are talking to; for this business of talking scandal is like a game of battledore and shuttlecock; either side feels bound to keep it up. You try it, next time somebody is ventilating his grievances to you; let him go on, don't agree with him, don't disagree with him; just retort with "Oh, really?" and "Is that so?", and you will be surprised to find how soon the conversation flags. And finally, if you air your discontentment in public, you do an injury to all your listeners by setting them, openly, a bad example. Most of our sins, you see, we are rather ashamed of; we feel fools, afterwards, if we have lost our temper in public; we don't like to be caught out telling a lie. But when we talk uncharitably we always imagine—too often, I'm afraid, with justice—that our company enjoys it. So much the worse if they do; you are lowering the standard of fraternal charity with every word you say; and, if you are talking in front of people younger than yourself or less important than yourself, you are setting them an example they will be only too ready to follow. Probably at your expense, you know, the moment you have left the room. How terrible it is to leave the room, when all the company has been exchanging uncharitable criticisms for the last hour or so!

And finally, by indulging this habit of murmuring you are spoiling in yourself the virtue of humility, the virtue of patience, and your own peace of mind.

The virtue of humility. What a fine fellow this self of ours is! How generous, how tactful, how considerate, what a man of the world! How efficiently, and yet how unostentatiously, he manages the work that is entrusted to him; how carefully he avoids infringing other people's rights; how edifying he manages to be, and at the same time how natural! And yet humility teaches us that we are not to regard this fine fellow as a finer fellow than his neighbours. Don't you see, then, that we ought to blind our eyes to the tactlessness, the incompetence, and all the other defects of those neighbours of ours? Otherwise the picture of this fine fellow will dominate our imagination too much. At all costs we must avoid comparisons; and how are we to avoid comparisons if half our conversation is devoted, day in day out, to the shortcomings of other people? That Pharisee in the temple would not have been guilty of the pride which sent him down to his house unjustified, if he hadn't caught sight, out of the corner of his eye, of that cringing publican beating his breast and making an exhibition of himself. No, we must turn our eyes away, resolutely, from other people's faults; it may give us time, you know, to observe that the fine fellow has some faults of his own.

The virtue of patience. Almighty God means us to suffer; it is good for us; and he means us to suffer not only from natural causes over which man has no control, but from our fellow-men; from the mistakes, the misjudgements, the misgovernment of our fellow-men. Most of us have some unlovable qualities which we can't help; most of us do and say the wrong thing, without meaning to; and besides that, there are our faults. Part of the reason why God put you into the world was to exercise the patience of others by your defects; think of that sometimes when you are going to bed. It is a salutary thought . . . Your bad temper, your excessive cheerfulness, your tiresomeness in conversation; he chose the right person, didn't he? Well, if other people are being so admirably exercised in patience by you, it seems a pity you shouldn't be exercised by them now and again in your turn; that's only fair. The offering of patience which you can make to God; the little things you have to put up with—and that offering is to be made in silence. How it spoils that offering if you make any comment on it, still more if you make any comment on it out loud, still more if you make any comment on it in the presence of other people! You must offer it to him like a casket of myrrh, not wasting the scent by opening the lid before it gets to him.

Your peace of mind. That's the one thing you can't afford to lose, next to your soul; even the Saints can't afford to lose that. Lose your peace of mind, and you lose your concentration of purpose, your capacity for recollection, your attentiveness to God's calls and inspirations. Now, a strong antipathy, like a strong attachment, does interrupt, if only for a short time, this peace of mind which is so precious to you; you cannot think calmly, you are swept away by gusts of resentment and self-pity, the grievance preys upon you, haunts you like a nightmare.

That is what happens, I mean, if you have really let murmuring get the upper hand in your life, and things are not going smoothly with you. Even worrying over trifles, how it can upset the poise and balance of the mind! Either those trifles concern you personally, or they don't. If they don't, then it is far better not to meddle in them at all; to tell yourself you are in danger of becoming a busybody, and leave them on one side. Or they do concern you personally,

and you are tempted to criticize somebody from whose con-
duct you yourself have to suffer. Believe me, you only add to
your grievance by taking it out for an airing. It is quite true
that it may do good to discuss it calmly with your confessor.
Or, very occasionally, it may be your duty to bring something to the notice of a person in higher authority. But to
chatter and gossip over your grievances never yet did any
good, never yet afforded any real relief; you only hypnotize
yourself into imagining your resentment to be stronger than
it really is. It is a conspiracy against your own peace of mind.

St. Thomas More, whose life was full of gracious customs,
had a quaint way of dealing with uncharitable conversation.
Whenever people began to indulge in it in his presence, he
used to break in suddenly and loudly, as if talking to himself: "They may say what they will, but I say that this house
is a good house, and the architect who built it is a clever
fellow". I don't mean that this formula would be equally
useful to all of us; there are presbyteries and religious houses
which it would not be possible to describe in that way without being suspected of paradox. But I think the holy man's
principle was absolutely sound—that if you want to put an
end to these sins of the tongue, you must start talking suddenly about something quite different. Have some fresh
topic of conversation up your sleeve, ready to be released
when people start exchanging grievances in your presence.
By such simple means, you may do more than you know to
preserve charity among your brethren, and win that special
title to God's sonship which is reserved for those who make
peace.

# 7

## ACCIDIE

When the people of Israel invaded, under
Josue, the territory of Chanaan, a Divine oracle gave them
directions about the treatment of the cities they were destined to conquer. And those directions have, before now,
been a puzzle to many of us. The inhabitants of these Cha-
naanitish cities must be put to the sword, apparently without
any distinction of age or sex. How (we naturally ask) could
the God of mercy whom we preach to-day issue, three thousand years ago, a command of savagery? How could he encourage his chosen people in taking such bitter measures
against their enemies? Were the Chanaanites so desperately wicked, all of them, was their stock so hopelessly de-
generate, that they had deserved nothing less in the way of
retribution? It may be so. For myself, saving the better
judgement of the Church, I have always been tempted to
imagine that the regulation we are speaking of was a prohibition, rather than a precept. In those days, I take it, and among
those fierce children of the desert, when you conquered a

country and settled down in it you took one or other of two alternative courses. Either you mixed with the conquered people, intermarried with them and fused your national traditions with theirs; or you exterminated them altogether, not sparing the women, who would introduce tamer blood into your own virile stock, not sparing the children, who might grow up to avenge their fathers later on. Since God wanted, above all things, to preserve his people from the debased and idolatrous worship which the Chanaanites practised, he forbade his people to adopt the milder alternative, and allowed their fiercer instincts to have free play. In the conditions of those barbarous times, he let rough justice take its course.

Whatever we think about the literal interpretation of these stories, their allegorical interpretation is surely plain and salutary. We Christians are engaged—that is the point—in a war of extermination against all that keeps us away from God.

What I want to call your attention to is a curious exception which had to be made when Josue carried out the command (or the prohibition) that was given him. The Gabaonites (if I may refresh your memory with the facts) realized that resistance to the invader was useless; realized, too, that surrender would only mean massacre, since they belonged to the doomed population of Palestine. They sent ambassadors, therefore, who pretended to come from a distant country; in ragged clothes, with worn-out shoes, with the very bread mouldering in their wallets, to create the impression of a long journey. And they succeeded in making a treaty with Josue, stipulating that their lives should be spared, since

they were ready to surrender at discretion; before Josue
found out who they really were, or where they really came
from. When the fraud was discovered, he could not go back
on his oath. He was directed to reduce the Gabaonites to the
position of slaves; temple slaves probably. They were to be
hewers of wood and drawers of water to the congregation of
Israel; and so (adds the chronicler) they remain to this day.

It may seem a strange flight of the imagination when I
find, in those Gabaonites who hewed wood and drew water
for the service of the temple, a parallel, and in some sort an
encouragement, for Christian people, and Christian people
who are called to the splendid career of the priesthood. But
bear with me for a moment while I explain my parable. I
think it is an experience not altogether uncommon, commoner certainly than the polite conventions allow us to admit, for a priest to wonder whether he has not, after all,
mistaken his vocation. Did God ever really mean him to be
a priest? Or did he mistake motives of human prudence, the
good opinion of his friends, some passing wave of enthusiasm, for the Divine call? There was, perhaps, a time during
his seminary course at which he felt scruples about it all, and
his confessor told him to disregard them, as scruples should
be disregarded; were they scruples? Did we, after all, impose
on the Bishop who ordained us, something as the Gabaonites
imposed on Josue? Did we make him believe that we had
left the world far behind us, when in truth it was still at our
elbow? To be sure, if we deceived others, we managed to
deceive ourselves equally; we did not act in conscious bad
faith. But, while that may extenuate our guilt, it does not
alter our mistake. We have become priests, when God never

called us to the priesthood. Miserable false step; how are we to retrieve it?

Understand me, reverend fathers; I am not referring to those tragedies of the priestly life which sometimes arise from a strong assault of temptation. God help us all, it might happen to any of us, in our mortal weakness, that a passion suddenly conceived, or long indulged through carelessness, should force us into a false position; a position in which great grace is needed to avert a disastrous decision. But I am not thinking, now, of these major perils. I am thinking, now, of what is (I fancy) much commoner; the position of a priest who has been, and remains, faithful to his promises of celibacy and of ecclesiastical obedience; there is no sudden crisis to be feared, and yet all is not well with him. Years have gone by, ten or twenty years maybe, since his ordination, and the first fervours have died away. It isn't that he doesn't do his job. He says his prayers, makes a preparation and thanksgiving of sorts, a meditation of sorts; he does all that could be expected of him to look after the souls put in his charge; but he does it all lifelessly. The Divine Office becomes more and more what the Church, in her grim realism, calls it—the office, the thing that gets in your way. He is concerned, not to say it, but to get it said. The Mass itself brings with it no feelings of awe, of mystery, of content. The care of souls, which he used to find so interesting, is now hand-over-hand work; they all seem to him much alike, much on a level, and not a very high level at that. All the savour has gone out of his priesthood; he sometimes thinks, even out of his religion. Was he, perhaps, not meant to be a priest? There are so many useful and unselfish things he

could be doing, in a sick world, if he weren't a priest. Is it
possible that he has made a mistake?

Now, don't let's be in too much of a hurry to blame ourselves over all that. One thing is lucidly obvious about human nature, and that is that the thrill of novelty does wear
off, and as you grow older you find less natural zest about
things which were once full of excitement and romance. It
happens, I suppose, to a more or less extent even in the most
successful of marriages. And it seems to me a very extraordinary thing that nobody ever warns young priests about this;
let me take this opportunity of warning those of you who
are only a few years out from the seminary. A great deal of
the thrill, a great deal of the interest which our priestly
duties give us at first is not supernatural, though we often
feel as if it was. A great deal of it is purely natural, purely
human. The Mass and the office interest us because of the
poetry in them, because of the mystery in them. We rather
enjoy—if the cruel truth must be told—dressing up and going through ceremonies in front of a watchful congregation;
if we are the kind of people who can do that sort of thing
well. Work for souls is, of all work, the most interesting, just
at first. And all that human satisfaction which we get out of
our priestly duties is a thing which fades away with the years;
it is inevitable. And this very obvious but seldom mentioned
fact, which is useful as a warning to the young priest, may be
useful as consolation to the priest who is getting on in
years. When you complain that your priestly life seems
mechanical and flat as compared with what it seemed ten
years ago, remind yourself in the first place that what you
have lost is, in great part, a merely human love of your job,

and love of doing your job well, which was bound to disappear in any case.

Yes, you say, that's all very well, but it's not quite my trouble. What I mind about is not so much that I seem to get so little out of my religion, but that I seem to put so little into it. Or perhaps I should put it in this way, what I mind about is that I should mind so little. Just when I'm in retreat like this, I feel ashamed of having so little love for God, so little zeal for the faith and for the Church; but when I'm back at my work, I'm conscious of all that, and I don't seem to care. I'm content to go on in this mechanical way, and remind myself that lots of other priests are probably in the same position. It isn't merely that my religion does nothing to arouse my feelings; what are feelings, after all? The trouble is that it doesn't really command the loyalty of my will. I'm afraid I don't make my meditation; or if I do, it's only a token meditation now and again. I find myself going onto the altar without having taken the trouble to prepare myself, deferring my office till the last possible moment. When I come across a soul which is hardened, ever so slightly, against the influence of religion, I just shrug my shoulders and say, "Well, if he won't, he won't; I can't help him". It isn't simply that I have got no taste for my job; I haven't got my heart in my job. And that, surely, is a matter of the will.

I know. That is the state, of course, which the spiritual authors call tepidity. If you ask me to suggest a remedy for that, I should be inclined to answer in two words, and those two words are "spiritual reading". I am afraid that sounds a dull prescription. It recalls unprofitable half-hours when you sat, as a divine or a novice, with Scaramelli open on your lap. I don't think it is important, when we do spiritual reading, that it should be something dull. On the contrary, we ought to take some trouble, more trouble than we ordinarily do, about finding an author whose style and whose outlook appeals to us. But having found our spiritual author, we should give him his head. Don't skip, don't stray about, don't tell yourself, "I think perhaps this is rather stiff going for a person like me". Read steadily on, with an open heart, and God will find the right passages to awaken your conscience where it is needed and as it is needed. You can say office year after year, you can repeat any number of formal prayers day after day, you can meditate, even, on approved lines, and yet never hear God's voice talking suddenly to your soul. Your prayer has become mechanized, and your mind, from long use, is shut to the implications of it. But spiritual reading is a splendid trap to catch souls. You are reading on, quite calmly, and all of a sudden a sentence flashes out of the page, and you say to yourself, "By Jove, that's true", and the next moment you say to yourself, "By Jove, that's me".

Having said so much about remedies, may I go back to where I was before, and point out, what is almost certainly true, that this tepidity of which you accuse yourself does go side by side with, and is partly caused by, the phenomenon we were talking about; I mean, a slackening off, not altogether due to your own fault, of your interest in spiritual things. That slackening off, with some of us, is a matter of age; with some, a matter of temperament; with some, a matter of circumstances—we are set down to do a dull job, which is not really our job, and we lose heart and grow disillusioned about what a vocation to the priesthood means. Very likely you complain that the work you have to do isn't worth doing, or isn't your work anyhow. Don't be too certain that that is the trouble. A doctor once told me—I don't know if it's true, but he was a very famous doctor—that you never ought to say you caught cold through sitting in a draught, because you don't feel a draught until you've already got a cold. And I think when a priest complains, not of difficulties in his work, but of the dull, dead level of his congregation, that that SOMETIMES is just due to the dull, dead level of the priest. But it is true, I think, that parish work, and a *fortiori* work on the foreign missions, *is* calculated to keep us up to the mark. And if for no fault of his own the priest who aspired to serve God in that way finds himself turned into a professor, it isn't the same thing. He misses that interplay of life with life, of mind with mind, which is a grace God ordinarily gives us, to keep us fresh and supple. But if that is part of the trouble, it is not, you admit, the whole of the trouble. The fact is (you say) that things seem to have gone very flat with me; and I should think that if I go through the motions of serving God, it's about all I do.

Yes. Well, there's something to be said for going through the motions of serving God. What I'm wanting to suggest, if there is anybody here who feels like that about it, is something rather bold, something that might even sound unorthodox if you stated it too crudely. You may think it has a smack of Quietism about it. I can only say that it is the best light I have, but I don't want anybody to pay any attention to it except in so far as it seems to him a right and reasonable attitude that I am recommending.

At to whether God meant you to be a priest, stop worrying. He certainly means you to be a priest now; your priesthood is contained, if not in his antecedent will, at least in his consequent will. You may have crept in under false pretences like the Gabaonites, but he is faithful to his word, and he promises us the graces we need for our state of life as long as we do our part. He wants you, now, to be a priest, and a good priest. But in the meanwhile the facts have got to be faced. There is this heavy tedium which you cannot shake off, that makes your whole priestly life feel dull and second-rate. You cannot, even under the search-light of a retreat like this, detect any grave fault which you can amend, any obvious sacrifice you can make to God, in the hope of improving the situation. You can only go on, doing your best to serve God, with the dispiriting consciousness that it is really only a second best, praying for greater fervour, for the rekindling of your love. In what spirit are you to undertake that difficult and ungrateful task?

That is where the Gabaonites come in. Tell Almighty God that he has, for whatever reason, made you, at least for the time being, a hewer of wood and a drawer of water in his service; it seems, for the moment, all you can aspire to; very well, you will perform this humble office, faithfully, to prove your love of him. You will go on doing that, if need be, all your life through; not complaining that he has appointed you to this destiny, as long as you can find no power in yourself to look higher. Make up as best you can, by your humility, and by a kind of dogged obedience, for all the priestly qualities he sees lacking in you.

You are preparing to go the altar. You feel certain that all will be as it was yesterday and the day before; there will be no conscious response in you to the sacred words of the liturgy, or even to the near approach of our blessed Lord as he comes to you in holy Communion. It will all be a mechanical routine, like filling in forms. Never mind; you are preparing to offer this lifeless performance to God, all the more hopefully because for you it is a thing without salt; you are doing it, not to please yourself but to please him. Jesus Christ, our high Priest, is going to offer himself in the Holy Mass, using you as his tool—his dull, uncomprehending tool; you will offer yourself, motionless, into his hands. You will be acting like a conscript soldier under orders, not buoyed up by any foretaste of victory, any consciousness of heroism, but simply doing what he is told. That shall be your sacrifice.

You take up the well-thumbed breviary, and arrange the tattered markers in it. You know well what your office is going to mean; a verse or two read with some sense of what the meaning is about, but alas, with no unction; then a long rumination on your own affairs, starting off at a wide tangent; then the bell that rings in your memory and recalls you to a sense of what you are doing; always the same. A parrot, you feel, would do it as well. To be sure, but at least you can take upon yourself the duties of God's parrot; the beasts, too, praise God. Tell him that all this mouthing of syllables is meant for his glory; you wish it could be something better, but ask him to accept that. You are making a meditation, or a visit to the Blessed Sacrament; why is it that your heart is dumb? You command an act of thanksgiving, or adoration, whatever it may be; nothing comes—there is no answer, in sensitive nature, to the call. You feel like a man trying to drive a mule, when the mule doesn't want to go. Well, there is that comforting verse in the Psalm, "I have become like a beast of burden in thy sight; I was reduced to mere nothingness, and was all ignorance". This nothingness, this ignorance, this blank which is all you have to offer in the way of prayer is something to offer; keep still before God in the consciousness and the confession of your own barrenness; reach out towards him, humbly, in the dark. You go out to visit some of your parishioners; what an opportunity for a priest with a real zeal for souls! With you, it will be a few courtesies of conversation, a shy hint about the abstract possibility of going to confession—nothing more. You, who ought to be a shepherd to these people, no better, it seems, than a finger-post! Still, you are a finger-post; the mere presence of a priest among them means something. It is for others to do great things for God; it is for you to offer to him the little good that is done by your ministry, asking him to make you useful somehow, perhaps without your knowing it, to the souls he wants to bring to himself through you.

God forgive me, if I have been encouraging any of you to acquiesce in low standards; that has not been my intention. All I mean is that during those intervals—please God, they are only intervals—in which our own want of progress whispers the temptation to despair, we should rather turn our own shortcomings into a motive for humility, and therefore into a means of grace. Prayer is essentially throwing yourself back upon God; and when you are going through a bad time spiritually, that may be the very best opportunity for throwing yourself back on him, with all the more abandonment because you feel you have nothing of your own to give him. It may be, this bad time was sent you for that purpose; if things had gone too smoothly with you, there would have been danger of taking pride in your own efforts. Lord (says the old prayer) if thou wishest me to be in the light, blessed be thy name; if thou wishest me to be in darkness, blessed be thy name. Light and darkness, bless ye the Lord.

# 8

# ON FEARING GOD

If you read through the Hebrew prophets from end to end—not many people do—the last of them, Malachy, strikes you with a sense of homeliness, and almost of modernity. Partly because, except for one verse, his book is intelligible throughout. But partly because he does not share with his fellow-prophets their apparent indifference to all the externals of religion. Of course, we quite realize that the Jews under the Old Dispensation needed to be warned against merely external religion; for that matter, we need it ourselves. But the prophets seem so obsessed with it; look at the way in which Amos represents Almighty God as talking to his people. "Oh, but I am sick and tired of them, your solemn feasts; incense that goes up from your assemblies I can breathe no longer. Burnt-sacrifice still? Bloodless offerings still? Nay, I will have none of them; fat be the victims you slay in welcome, I care not. O to be rid of the singing, the harp's music, that dins my ear!" Well, some of us aren't too happy about our own choirs; and apart from that, we

know that the Israelites of Amos' time were worshipping
Moloch on the side and oppressing the poor. But you can't
[help feeling that a diocesan censor would have recom-
mended the prophet to phrase it rather differently.

With Malachy, you leave all that behind you. For him,
there is one glaring reason why Almighty God is discontented with his people; it is because the priests are not doing their job. In particular, they are allowing people who
offer sacrifice to bring the worst of their cattle with them
instead of the best. At first sight, you would think that was
the fault of the laity; after all, it was the priests had to eat
what was left over. . . . But no, it was the priests' job to
teach people the law, which laid it down expressly that the
victim of any statutory sacrifice must be a perfect animal,
without blemish. And the priests weren't doing that, apparently because they had come to treat the whole of the
Temple worship with disdain.

I suppose it was at the time when the people had just
come back from exile, and were living in pre-fabricated build-
ings, and everything was rather utility; the temple itself, old
people would tell you, was a very poor substitute for the old
one. And in the general atmosphere of disillusionment, the
priests had got disillusioned too; shrugged their shoulders
and said well what could you expect. "You think to yourselves, The Lord's table is desecrated now; it makes no
matter what food lies there, what fire burns it. Weary work,
say you, and dismiss it with a sigh. Cursed be the knavery
that offers the Lord gelt beast, when there are vows a-paying,
and all the while there is an entire beast left at home! Offers
it to the Lord of hosts, the great king, no name in all the

world so terrible. It is for you, priests, to see that this law of mine is obeyed." *Mutatis mutandis* there is, as I say, something curiously modern about it; you might easily mistake it for a rather sharp pastoral letter. And when the prophet goes on to denounce mixed marriages, that does nothing to dispel the illusion.

It would be easy, *mutatis mutandis*, to give you a meditation on the main theme of Malachy's protest. The poor Jew, fresh from years of exile, who found that the latest lamb in his flock was a miserable-looking specimen, and said, before he realized what he was saying, "That one looks as if it would do for the Lord of hosts"—can we really cast a stone at him? Aren't we too conscious of the lag in our own spiritual lives, when the Lord of hosts asked us for our best, and we gave him our second best, if that—the half-hearted sacrifice, the scamped job, the difficulty pushed aside when it ought to have been faced? But I thought I would draw your attention to a different aspect of Malachy's teaching, one, indeed, which is common to him and to all his fellow-prophets—his insistence on the *fear* of God. "The Lord of hosts, the great king, no name in all the world so terrible"; it is not so much the want of generosity that surprises him, as the want of salutary fear. He admits, to be sure, that there is another side to it. "Son to father, servant to master gives his due; your father I, where is the honour, your master I, where is the reverence you owe me?" Yes, ungrateful sons, but, almost more evidently, foolhardy servants defying their master's displeasure. The love of God is a phrase almost unknown to the Old Testament; the prophets call upon Israel not to love God but to fear him. Now for the reverse side of the medal; open your concordance again, and you find that the New Testament writers talk to us about loving God, not fearing him. If you cut out the references in Acts to "those who feared God", which is only a technical name for the Gentile proselytes who had adopted Jewish worship, if you cut out Old Testament quotations, how many times do the authors of the new dispensation urge us to fear God? About a dozen times, not more. The emphasis has exactly changed. Israel's worship was fear with an undercurrent of love, ours is love with an undercurrent of fear.

But the fear is still there. Our Lord, as we know, warns us to fear the God who can destroy both body and soul in hell. St. Paul tells us that we must achieve the work of our sanctification in the fear of God, and, more surprisingly, encourages husband and wife to respect one another's rights "in the fear of Christ". And to this day, when we catechize our people, we enumerate the seven gifts of the Holy Spirit as Isaias enumerated them, ending up with "the fear of the Lord". Fear *has* a place in Christian spirituality.

What place? We mustn't disguise from ourselves the fact that there is a difficulty here. Our Lord, you see, almost expressly reverses the language of Malachy. "Your father I, where is the honour, your master I, where is the reverence you owe me?"—that was the old basis of appeal, but our Lord seems to revise it: "I do not speak of you any more as my servants; a servant is one who does not understand what his master is about; . . . I have called you my friends". St. Paul catches up the utterance as a slogan of emancipation; "No longer then art thou a slave, thou art a son"; and, more explicitly, "The spirit you have now received is not, as of old, a spirit of slavery, to govern you by fear; it is the spirit of adoption, which makes us cry out, Abba, Father!" And St. John is even more definite about it: "Love has no room for fear; and indeed, love drives out fear when it is perfect love, since fear only serves for correction. The man who is still afraid has not yet reached the full measure of love". From such passages as those you might easily infer that love is the specific motive of all Christian action, and no other can be accepted as a tolerable substitute. And I think you would probably find that many well-meaning theologians, outside the radius of the Church's influence, do teach exactly that. Fear of any kind, they would tell you, is a morbid affection of the human psyche, and exists only to be got rid of. A theology which insists upon hell is out of keeping with a civilization which wants to get rid of capital punishment.

I don't think we shall get much help from our own theologians here. Their chief interest in the subject is a rather squalid argument with the Lutherans about attrition, and whether it is all right to repent of your sins out of servile fear, as long as it is *simpliciter servilis* and not *serviliter servilis*. The subject of fear itself doesn't seem to interest them much. So I think we may be allowed to make a few distinctions of our own, without feeling that we are trespassing on their preserves. It isn't, after all, a matter of dogma we are discussing; it is a matter of spiritual emphasis. How big ought the fear of God to loom in our consciousnesses? "O, how I fear thee, living God, with deepest, tenderest fears"—there's Father Faber at it again; is he exaggerating, as Father Faber sometimes exaggerates? We want to get the thing in the right perspective, that's all.

Well, in the first place I would suggest this; we ought to fear God, but not to be frightened of God. Mr. Belloc, as he so often does, makes a good distinction there: "Fear I think, indeed, to be in the nature of things; but terror, which is a sudden madness and paralysis of the soul, that I say is from hell, and not to be played with or considered or put in pictures or described in books". There are people with whom fear is, unmistakably, a morbid affection, and there are people with whom the fear of God is a morbid affection; I mean, the scrupulous. A wrong adjustment between fear of God and trust in God, that is all scruples are; but they do exist, and heaven knows they are hard to deal with. So let's concede that much to our Protestant friends; to be frightened of God, to have a morbid fear of him, is a bad thing. And incidentally, if we are in the habit of preaching hell-fire sermons—most of us aren't—let's remember that there are three scrupulous people in the parish and they will all be there.

Another point; we ought to fear God, but we oughtn't to be afraid of God. To be afraid of a thing is to run away from the subject, try and blot it out of your mind. And, what's worse, you don't do it deliberately, you do it without knowing that you are doing it. And I think, in various forms, being afraid of God is rather common. Sometimes it means, especially with young people, sin leading to infidelity; unrepented sin makes the thought of God a subject they are anxious to avoid, but they don't admit it to themselves, they go on pushing away, pushing away the thought of God all the time without knowing that they are doing it, until at last it just isn't there. But you get the same sort of thing,

I fancy, in the minds of quite ordinary people, who are living, at least on the surface, quite ordinary Christian lives. The thought of God makes them feel uncomfortable; all that business about eternity, and invisibility, and not occupying a position in space; he's too big to get inside their telescope. And so they take refuge in devotions to our Lord and devotions to our Lady and the blessed Saints *instead*; all those lovely devotions which are meant to make it easier to think about God are, for them, a set of pious distractions which allow them to think about something else. And it does make you wonder if that isn't what's wrong with some of those people who are so full of pieties and yet never seem full of piety. Nothing is more certain than that we degrade religion if we let people think of Almighty God merely as a terrifying figure in the background, throwing into relief, by his awful unapproachableness, the tender human appeal of our Lord and his Saints. God is there to be loved.

Well then, where exactly *does* fear come in? There's one ready-made solution of the difficulty, which I've no doubt has been occurring to many of you; much of the language used by the spiritual authors would seem to lend colour to it. It's this; that fear is meant for the half-hearted Christian, love for the perfect Christian. After all, it takes all sorts to make a Church; there will always be weaker brethren, incapable (apparently) of any great generosity, unmoved by any appeal to the tender emotions, who have nevertheless got the faith and mean, if they can manage it, to save their souls. Very well then, if the love of God isn't a sufficiently powerful motive, with them, to keep them out of sinful habits, or to produce repentance when they have sinned, let the fear of God do it instead. To be sure, they will always be rather Grade II Christians; but God is very merciful, and they will scrape through somehow, as long as they evince some signs of compunction more gracious than the bare fear of hell. The fear of God is not a very high motive, but it's a useful second-best.

I wonder, is that really good psychology? Or anyhow, is it suited to the age and the country in which we live? You see, if there is any truth in what I was saying just now about the sinner being afraid of God and consequently trying to run away from the thought of him, the threat of punishments in a future life may have exactly the wrong effect, instead of the effect you intended. He lives in a society which has largely gone heathen, which openly scoffs at the idea that any such punishments exist. How little is needed, to throw him into the arms of the free-thinker! Even the careless Christian, is it our experience that the appeal to fear will pull him up, commonly at least, when the appeal to love has failed? And, in any case, can we really be satisfied with the notion that the gift of fear, one of the seven gifts of the Holy Ghost, one of the seven gifts which are to descend, mark you, on the Christ himself, is only meant for one set of Christians, and those the least admirable?

No, it won't do. It won't do, I think, even if you revise the form of your suggestion, and say that the gift of fear is meant to keep good Christians out of sin at certain moments; moments of passion, when the love of God has become obscured in our minds and we want some more violent check to hold us back. The fear of God must be something more important, surely, than the net which hangs under the tight-rope in case the acrobat should fall. And what is all this about keeping us out of sin? Nothing is more depressing than the habit we all have, if we are not careful, of talking about religion as if it were a dodge for avoiding sin. Religion is man offering to God the highest worship of which a rational creature is capable. And the gifts of the Holy Ghost are not seven different recipes for avoiding sin. They are seven facets which shine out on the perfect jewel of Christian sanctity.

Perhaps we could put the thing more justly by altering the metaphor. Could we put it in this way, that fear of God is the salt of a fully developed spirituality? Not a food exactly; books of devotion do not, commonly at least, encourage us to make an act of fear. No, but a kind of spice which brings out, instead of destroying, the flavour of our sacrifice. You know how, after some hair-breadth escape, when you have just managed to keep your footing (say) in a place where losing it might have meant death, the thrill of fear still pulses in you, side by side with the overwhelming access of relief; and the two instincts, so far from contradicting one another, seem to merge into one another—fear actually lends an edge to the sense of relief. So it ought to be, surely, when you and I make an act of confidence in the goodness of God. *Misericordiae Domini quia non sumus consumpti;* the gratitude we feel for our preservation is only accentuated by the contemplation of that gulf into which we so nearly slipped, that gulf which still yawns beneath us. So, too, with our acts of love. They are artificial, because they are selective, if we think only of the kindness which has pardoned us. At the back of our minds, we should have a consciousness of the justice which might have cast us away. The Object of our love is a God of terrors, who might have rejected us, and would still be worthy of that love we should then be refusing him. Moses, at the burning bush, must take the shoes off his feet before he approached; there can be no encounter with Deity which does not claim its tribute of dread.

Understand me, I don't mean to suggest that the thought of hell ought to be present to our minds, or even present at the back of our minds, all the time we are at prayer. You might as well suggest that it was impossible to make an act of love to God without thinking about heaven. No, the meditation of God's goodness to us in granting us an eternal reward is meant to lead us on to the reflection, how good God is in himself. In the same way, surely, the meditation of God's severity towards the impenitent sinner is meant to lead us on; lead us on to the reflection how great God is in himself; positive Justice, incommunicable Holiness. In that sense, if you like, the meditation of hell is for beginners. Hell is only the demonstration of the Divine Justice, and the Divine Justice considered in itself is the true motive for our fear of God. Enough that we should approach him with awe; there is no need for us to itemize his terrors.

May I add, that this posture of approach is particularly demanded of us priests? Partly because, when all is said and done, the faithful so largely take their cue from us; "Ay, says the Lord of hosts, the guilt is yours"; don't let us forget Malachy's reminder. Did it ever occur to you that each of the letters which waits for you on your breakfast-table describes you, on the envelope, as a man who ought to inspire awe? And we shall not be reverenD fathers unless we are reverenT fathers first. And also because, obviously enough, we priests are more tempted to irreverence, in church at any rate, than the congregation are. We are behind the scenes all the time; there is no distance to lend enchantment to the view. We can see the damp patch on the sanctuary wall, they can't; we are distracted for the hundredth time by the smirking look on the faces of those plaster angels which look so impressive from the body of the church; perhaps there is a spot or two of candle-grease on the altar-cloth; one of the altar-boys has a cold, and has neglected to provide himself with a handkerchief. We are tempted to hurry over the Mass, remembering other people's breakfasts; we are tempted to say the words in a rather off-hand, detached way, for fear of seeming affected or sanctimonious. One way or another, there is a tendency, isn't there, for us to get rather slap-dash, rather casual, about our appearances in church; and, you know, I think there is a danger of that kind of external irreverence working inwards, and actually creating in our minds a certain disrespect for the things of God. We need, sometimes, the warning which Malachy gave to the priests of his own day: "Ask you, what care was lacking, when the bread at my altars is defiled? Ask you what despite you have done me, when you hold the Lord's table a thing of little moment?" . . . "The Lord of hosts, the great king, no name in all the world so terrible".

How little they matter, the external things! And yet, how little can be made of us, if we don't get even the external things right!

# 9

# ABANDONMENT

I wonder if you find, as I do, that spiritual reading comes easier in French than in English? The reason being, that so much of the world's best spirituality comes from France; and that even when you get a reasonably good translation (which you very seldom do), there are certain words in the vocabulary of French piety which have no natural equivalent in English. Such a word is abandon, the slogan (as people call it nowadays) of Père de Caussade.

The nearest word, perhaps, is "resignation"; but what a feeble rendering! We have used it, like so many other words in the English language, in a hundred trivial contexts, until its native force seems to have been lost altogether. "Very well", you say, "I'm resigned"; you accompany the remark with a shrug of the shoulders, indicating that it is no use quarrelling with the inevitable. Had you been consulted, had your advice been taken, at an earlier stage in the proceedings, things wouldn't ever have got into such a terrible mess, but it's too late to think of that now; very well, you are re-

signed. As usual, other people's interests have been considered, not yours; it is to be hoped that the arrangements made
will suit them, because for you nothing could possibly be
more inconvenient; no matter, you are resigned. How is a
word like "resignation", with these overtones of ungracious
acquiescence, to do duty for *abandon*, that ecstasy of self-
surrender in which the soul of the devout Christian throws
itself back upon God?

This attitude of surrender I take to be a thing of the first
importance, not only for souls living very close to God, but
for the average Christian; and that at all times. There is no
life so cushioned with ease, so hedged about with conven-
tion, that tragedy may not blunder into it suddenly, all un-
announced, regardless of the proprieties. A moment of acute
embarrassment for the onlooker, if I may put it in that way,
when disaster on a great scale obtrudes itself into the life
of somebody who has never, all his life, thought about the
will of God! How inadequate the receiving instrument
seems to be! But there are times when the pressure of public
events overclouds the outlook even of the most selfish, even
of the most thoughtless. There is but a step, we feel, between us and death; an unforeseen, uncontrollable turn of
affairs may plunge our whole world into chaos, may strike at
every life that is dear to us. This haunting preoccupation
at the back of our minds interferes with all our daily inter-
course, makes prayer a Purgatory of distractions. Then, if
we have not learned to abandon ourselves to God, how shall
we do? We are shut up in the dark with our despairs.

What is the precise nature of this act or attitude by which
we throw ourselves, utterly and (as we hope) irrevocably on

God? There are two quite different ways of looking at it, neither of which, taken by itself, seems to add up. Is it to be an act of confidence, by which we tell ourselves and God that we are sure he will bring us safely out of all our dangers? Or is it to be an act of self-immolation, by which we tell God that we don't mind whether we come safely out of our dangers or not?

In Holy Scripture, I think you can say that the emphasis is always laid on an act of confidence. All through the Psalms this note of trust in God is continually recurring; you might almost say that trust in God is what the Psalms are about. And so it is all through the Old Testament, but always with the understanding that God will deliver us from whatever dangers surround us, if we trust him sufficiently. Obviously it is one of the principal points in the teaching which our Lord gave to his apostles; St. Peter ought to have known that he couldn't sink, the boat's crew ought to have known that the boat couldn't founder, if they only had faith. And St. Peter, learning his lesson from such experiences as that, has passed it on to us. "Throw back on him" he tells us "the burden of all your anxiety; he is concerned for you". That God looks after his own, and will not let their cause go by default, even in this world, is a notion that has inspired lovers of the gospel in all ages, sometimes almost to the point of fanaticism. You read, for example, of the Moravian Brethren, an eighteenth-century sect who were energetic in conducting foreign missions, that they wished "the Brotherhood had one or two ships of its own, so that their immunity from sea risks might advertise to the world our Saviour's hand upon his people". No insuring at Lloyd's for them, you see; ships owned and manned by the servants of the gospel would, quite evidently, be unsinkable.

Well, no doubt there is danger of superstition there; our Lord would not accept Satan's challenge to jump off from the Temple roof. And there is danger, perhaps, of a certain smugness, when you begin to tell yourself that you are under God's special protection, almost assuming at the back of your mind that other people are not. But when all is said and done, we are committed, as Christians, to the doctrine of Providence. God does watch over every one of us, and so orders our lives that everything conspires together for good; if we make the right use of our opportunities, nothing can happen to us that will not conduce to our advantage, here or hereafter. To throw yourself into the arms of Providence, with the sure conviction that everything will turn out for the best, is an attitude nobody can quarrel with, as far as it goes. The only question is, whether it goes far enough? Is that *all* the spiritual authors mean when they talk about self-abandonment?

I think it is quite certain that some of them mean more than that. You see, to throw yourself back upon God because you feel quite certain he will protect you if you do, demands a great deal of faith, but it doesn't demand a great deal of generosity. You are, after all, doing what is the best thing for yourself. Aren't you making a kind of bargain with God, promising him your confidence if he will give you, in return —well, if not a happy life here, at least a happy eternity? What the mystics recommend to us is a more intimate kind of abandonment; they want us to abandon ourselves to the Divine will so utterly, so regardlessly, that we forget all about our own happiness, even about the happiness of heaven. This attitude, I need hardly say, was very much exaggerated by the Quietists of the seventeenth century. By their way of it, a soul ought to be so absorbed in the will of God that it would be a kind of infidelity even to wonder whether you were going to be saved or not. We have the record of a priest, belonging to this school of piety, who actually died praying God to send him to hell, as a just punishment for his sins. It is no wonder that, at the end of the century, these pedantries of devotion incurred a formal censure at Rome.

The God we Christians worship is a God of mercy and pardon; you must not represent him as a Juggernaut, riding roughshod over the victims of his justice, and demanding their acquiescence. But when you have cleared away the exaggerations, it remains true that self-abandonment has been preached by writers of undoubted orthodoxy in the sense of total self-abandonment, giving yourself up to God without any reserves or afterthoughts; not asking what destiny, joy or sorrow, is to be yours in this world, not overcurious about the destiny that is to be yours in eternity. Which is the right attitude, then, for you and me, as far as God gives us the grace to abandon ourselves? An attitude of confidence that all will be well with us? Or an attitude of indifference, which prefers to leave everything to him?

I wonder. Do you think it's possible that when we ask that question we are making the mistake of trying to analyse too much, rationalize too much? I rather suspect that there is a mood or attitude which comes quite natural to us, to the Saints all the time, to you and me part of the time, of want-

ing to throw one's hand in and let Almighty God take control
instead—without ever asking ourselves why we want that,
or what we expect to be the result of it. When I call it a
mood or an attitude, I don't mean to imply (as the words
might seem to imply) that it is unreal or transient. It isn't
just the result of low spirits or of indigestion; it isn't a sort
of compensation or escape which we devise for ourselves
when we feel left out of things. No, it's something which is
quite as likely to occur in our moments of triumph as in our
moments of defeat. I call it a mood or an attitude, in the
sense that it is not something we have thought up for ourselves by any series of pious considerations; it is not a deliberate act of the will which we make because we think we
ought to make it. No, it is a realization which seems to come
over us without any effort on our part, and I think it is a grace.
It is somehow borne in upon us that all our judgements,
the judgements we make for ourselves, are simply meaning-
less; that all our actions, the actions we do for our own human motives, are simply worthless. We become ciphers instead of units in the scheme of creation; we look in the look-
ing-glass, and find that we are not there. Everything is out of
focus until it is focussed not in ourselves, but in God. And
in that mood we fall back upon him, and tell him that we
are going to leave everything in his hands; we can find no
rest until we rest in him.

If we go to the philosophers, and ask them to prove to us
the existence of God, one of their submissions is, that there
must be Something which exists necessarily, exists in its own
right, and this is not true of anything in that outer world
which is perceived by the senses. Everything in the material

universe has a merely contingent existence; it just happens to be there, but it might just as well have been something else, might just as well not have been there at all. The argument is so rarefied that it makes our heads spin a little; we look out of the window at a bird singing on a tree, and dutifully assure ourselves that the tree might just as well have been a telegraph pole, that the bird might just as well not have existed. But (unless we are very metaphysically minded) the argument does not come home to us until we apply it to ourselves. Is *my* existence necessary? Do *I* exist in my own right? We have only to ask the question to see that the answer is No. And yet, if I have an argument with somebody, I go away convinced that he is wrong and I am right—I, not he, must be the centre of existence. If the whole world goes to war, I try hard to think of all the people who will be inconvenienced by it in various ways; but what I am really thinking about is how it will affect *me* and the people *I* personally am fond of; *I* alone am treated as the centre of existence. So important we feel when we don't think about it, so unimportant the moment we do think about it; is it wonderful that this sudden loss of balance in our own esteem should make us want to fall back upon God?

Fall back upon him, not precisely with the object of finding protection in the hour of danger, comfort in our troubles, guidance in our difficulties. It is a more instinctive, a less calculating gesture than that; the equilibrium which has been lost must somehow be recovered, and we know there is no other way of recovering it, but in God. There is no time to ask for guarantees or to strike bargains; when the internal front has crumbled, there is nothing for it but unconditional surrender. In the logic of the thing, your first step must be to give yourself into God's hands unreservedly, not asking whether he has any use for you or any prospects for you, but simply handing yourself over as so much scrap, to be disposed of.

What happens afterwards is, I suppose, a matter of temperament; or perhaps we ought to say a matter of vocation; or perhaps we ought to say that it does not make much difference which word we use. There are some souls in which the act of surrender gives rise to a wave of buoyant optimism; not the foolish optimism of inexperience, but a grounded confidence in the forces that work with them. God has a place for them to fill, a work for them to do, on however small a scale; it may be the reducing of a parish debt, it may be the rescuing of one soul from indifference, that is the job allotted to them; but because they have identified themselves with the designs of Providence, instead of choosing for themselves, it is certain that Providence will not let them down. Difficulties exist only to be overcome; discouragement is only sent to be a trial of our faith; if God be for us, who can be against us? We can do all things through Christ who strengthens us. And sometimes, there is no denying it, if you merely judge by results, this strong trust in Providence is rewarded by the most extraordinary interferences of Providence on man's behalf; until we are tempted to think of self-abandonment merely as a policy which justifies itself, a matter of quid pro quo—as if God were bound in mere fidelity to reward us with success, and with conscious happiness, the moment we give up our wills to him.

But of course that won't do. God's mercies are free mercies still, even when we have done everything we could do to deserve them. And when we abandon ourselves to him, protest to him that we are nothing and claim nothing from him, are giving ourselves to him so that he can do what he likes with us, is he never to take us at our word? You cannot read far in the history of God's dealings with souls before you come across instances in which he has done so. He accepts our offering, and leaves us none the wiser; we remain fixed in a posture of self-abandonment without any means of guessing that *he* has not abandoned us too. For years St. Francis of Sales was convinced that he was destined to eternal perdition; for years he went on all the same quietly serving God, for love of him and not for any hope of reward.

That is an extreme case; but it is not, I think, at all uncommon to be left altogether unconsoled, when you have made your act of surrender; to lean upon God without any consciousness of support, to lose yourself without finding him. Without telling us why, he wants us to go on stretching out our hands towards him in the dark; the exercises of religion have no attraction for us, we can chart no record of progress or growth in our lives, even the  attitude of self-abandonment is no longer accompanied by any sweetness, any sense of relief. We seem held to it by some power outside ourselves, that will not let us go back on it. And there is worse. In an age like ours, so full of questionings and of false philosophies, the mind which is not comforted by any relish in the practice of religion is exposed, as on a bare nerve, to the chilling airs of doubt. It does not lose faith, but the clearness of its convictions is dimmed; it maintains itself by an effort, instead of basking in the sunshine of assured belief.

That, too, the Saints have known; at the end of her life St. Theresa of Lisieux suffered, to the last, this obscuration of belief. God wanted her, in this as in other ways, to be the Saint of our age.

We must take courage, then, and not be too ready to believe that all goes amiss with us, if we do not experience, in spite of the honest attempt to give ourselves to God, that lightness of heart and joy in his service which others, differently constituted and perhaps called to a different vocation, seem to regard as the natural consequence of their surrender. Perhaps they even tend to shake their heads over us, and suspect that we are on a wrong path; if we would listen to them, read their favourite authors, come and hear their favourite preacher, it would do us all the good in the world. It may be so; but more probably their vocation is not ours; God has called them to light, and us to darkness. We do well to confess that our own sins, our own infidelity to grace, have made us unworthy of any other treatment at God's hands. It may be so, but more probably God meant us for this, meant this for us; it is his way of dealing with us, and we must accept the drudge's task of living by an obscure faith which feeds, but does not inspire us.

# 10

## OBEDIENCE

(*To Seminarists Nearing Ordination*)

Shall we say something about obedience? A difficult, and rather an awkward subject. Is obedience a virtue? When we are quite small, we get the impression that it is the only virtue. When somebody says "Go upstairs and change your pinafore", if we go upstairs at once, without asking why our present pinafore won't do, without hanging about and playing with the cat on the way to the door, then we are a good child; our position is made. Of course, there are plenty of well-meaning people nowadays who think one ought never to tell a child to do anything, because it will have a bad effect on its psyche; one ought to say "Darling, there's a nice clean pinafore waiting for you upstairs; don't you think you would look rather smart in it?" But on the whole that sort of thing happens in books more than in real life; most of us, when we are quite small, are expected to do as we are told. And then we go to school, and there are still a lot of notices pinned up about changing our shoes and this

and that; and when we remember, we drift into an attitude
of dazed compliance with these regulations, except when we
can't be bothered. Even when we can't be bothered, we
don't feel it as a grievance that older people should pin up
notices like that; we are vaguely conscious that it would be
impossible to run a school without some kind of discipline,
so we suppose it's all right. Then we leave school; and it
suddenly becomes a question whether we ever need obey
anybody any more. It's true that in the Protestant wedding-
service the bride is supposed to undertake that she will obey
her husband; but I think they generally leave that part out
nowadays, and the Church, with her greater sense of realities,
says nothing about it at all. Obedience, for us, is finished
from now on.

And then the reflection occurs to us, "If obedience is really
a virtue, why is it that only children are lectured about it,
and only people of school age are expected to practise it?"
Father Sebastian Bowden, of the Oratory, told me once of a
middle-aged man who hadn't been anything out of the way
pious but was a quite decent Catholic; only now that he was
getting on in life he felt he ought to do something more
about it. So he came to Father Sebastian and asked him
about the Little Oratory, which is the sodality they keep
for lay people. Father Sebastian was delighted, and told him
all about the pious practices they had at the Little Oratory
meetings, and the man said, "Beautiful, beautiful". And
then he told him about all the indulgences that were at-
tached to these things, and the man said, "Wonderful, wonderful". And then Father Sebastian explained that the brothers of the Little Oratory took the discipline twice a week,

and the man said, "It sounds just the thing for my boy Tom".

Grown-up people—what have they got to do with discipline? All right in the fighting forces, you've got to have it there; but there, after all, it's only drill; it's not a virtue. We are told in a general way that we ought to obey the laws, and the civil power, but it's a curious thing that when people start disobeying the laws and the civil power, as long as it doesn't happen to be inside the British Commonwealth, we always say, "Splendid! I like to see people sticking up for their liberties. How hateful it must be to live under a dictatorship, and not be able to rebel whenever you want to!" Even inside the British Commonwealth we usually have a conference or a royal commission and give the people most of what they're asking for. As for the idea that a workman has any sort of duty to obey his employers, that has become hopelessly old-fashioned; of course you down tools the moment you don't like the orders you are given. The love of liberty, that is what we admire; if people obey orders, it's only because they can't be bothered.

And so we reach the conclusion that obedience isn't a virtue at all; it's only a kind of graceful accomplishment which we learn when we are young, but aren't expected to keep up, like skipping. And then suddenly we are confronted with the fact of the religious orders. Here are men and women all over the world, a great number of Christian people, and on the whole the pick of the bunch, deliberately binding themselves by life vows of poverty, chastity and obedience. Obedience—they go back into a sort of holy second childhood, in which they are not their own masters any longer; they don't have to make any decisions for themselves, only toe the line as it is marked out for them by their superiors. Not quite as thoroughly as the lay sister when the priest said, "It's a lovely day, isn't it?" and she said, "I'll go and ask Reverend Mother". But there it is; you actually find a whole crowd of people giving up their own wills and practising obedience for the love of God; surely there must be something in it after all?

Of course, you may say that obedience isn't exactly a virtue, it's a state of life; just as poverty isn't a virtue, only a state of life. But the *spirit* of obedience, anyhow, is a virtue canonized by the Church; if you doubt that, you have only to read through one of those dreary old-fashioned biographies of the Saints, where each virtue has a separate chapter to itself; and you will be sure to find one chapter, generally a rather long one, about the holy man's spirit of obedience. Now, it is obvious that the religious orders are meant to set us worldly people an example; the way they live is the kind of way we ought somehow to live, only they do it more thoroughly, and as it were in a professional way. The example of the holy religious, going through all their tremendous drill of sanctity day after day, isn't meant to depress us with a sense of our own inferiority. It's meant to encourage us in imitating, as and when our circumstances allow it, the spirit of obedience in which their lives are lived.

The spirit of obedience—you see, during our school-days obedience was there all over the place; bells were ringing, and notices were put up on the board, and we were sent on errands, and we did our prep for fear of what would happen if we didn't; but, was the spirit of obedience there? Wasn't there a certain tendency to break the rules, and even a certain unholy joy about breaking the rules, if it was pretty certain that you wouldn't be found out? And even when you did what you were told, wasn't there a temptation to do it rather slowly, rather grudgingly, keeping very strictly to the letter of your instructions, so as not to take an ounce more trouble than was absolutely necessary? Now and again, perhaps, when you had had a jawing from somebody you respected, you had a sort of pious fit which made you actually *want* to keep the rules; but it probably didn't last long. Well, it was quite natural that it should be so; in every school that I ever knew there is a kind of cold war going on all the time between the pupils and the people in authority, and in practice both sides recognize it. And you go to Christian doctrine class, and hear all about penal laws and how they aren't imposed on pain of mortal sin; and if the teacher is honest he explains to you that the rule about putting out your light at a certain time is a law of that description. So you keep the rules more or less, but you don't keep them in a spirit of obedience. "It's all a silly lot of fuss" you say to yourself; "but anything for a quiet life". Which is not, if you come to think of it, what the holy religious say about their holy rule.

Well, it's not difficult to see what I'm getting at. The seminarist is a sort of compromise, a rather uncomfortable compromise, between the school-boy and the novice; between the school-boy who obeys because it will jolly well be the worse for him if he doesn't, and the novice who obeys because obedience is the choice of his life-time—he wants to have everything arranged for him by superiors, so that he can be free to give himself without interruption to God. To put it in another way, the school-boy is supposedly being trained through discipline in order that he may become, at the age of seventeen, a responsible person, capable of looking after himself without interference from his elders. Whether this ideal is fully realized, either at Eton or at Borstal, is quite another question, but we needn't go into it; that is the theory of the thing. The school-boy is deprived of liberty for a time in order that he may be able to use it properly when he gets it. The novice, on the contrary, although the rules of the novitiate may be stricter than the rules of religion in general, is being trained in habits of obedience, so that he may go on obeying without a murmur all the rest of his life. Anyhow, that is the theory of the thing. Now, where exactly does the seminarist come in? Is he being trained through habits of discipline in order that he may become, at the age of twenty-five, a responsible person, capable of looking after himself without interference from his elders? Or is he being trained to habits of obedience, so that he may go on obeying rectors, and rural deans, and Vicars-general, and bishops, all the rest of his life?

The answer, I'm sorry to say, is "Betwixt and between". No doubt you are wondering why I give this meditation to you who are soon to be ordained, and not to *all* the divines. For two reasons, I think. One is, that I imagine you get conferences on the subject of obedience about twice a week from your superiors. And the other is that one can't do much, in the course of a single meditation, either to allay the scruples of the man who takes rules too literally, or to curb the adventurousness of the man who doesn't take them literally enough. But I wanted to say something to you about obedience, because you are nearing that uncomfortable parting of the ways when your whole attitude towards obedience comes up, necessarily, for revision. On the one hand, when you go out on to the mission you accept the responsibilities of a grown man. You have to decide for yourself whether you will accept this invitation or that, whether you will take up this hobby or that, whether you will read such-and-such a book or not; you can no longer dispose of the difficulty by the simple formula, "I don't think they'd want me to do that". On the other hand, you have not finished with the duty of submission to superiors; you are part of the cadre of Christ's army, and discipline is expected of you. In what spirit are you going to meet that situation?

It's forty-four years now since I was ordained as a clergyman of the Church of England. The head of my College gave me on that occasion, rather pointedly, I thought, a book called *The Spirit of Discipline*. I'm sorry to say that I still haven't read it. What impressed itself more on my mind was a meditation given during the ordination retreat, in which the preacher referred to an old countrywoman he once knew who always pronounced the word, not "DIScipline", but "disCIpline". He said he thought that was a fortunate error on her part, because after all that's what discipline really is—disciplin', being a disciple. The disciple, our Lord told us, is not greater than his Master; and, if you come to think of it, what a lot of discipline there was in our Lord's life! Think of the supernatural powers he enjoyed, and then reflect how seldom he used them. He could walk on the sea whenever he liked, but he went through all the inconveniences of a journey by boat except on this one occasion which was different. How he controlled himself; you might almost say, how he cramped himself! For him, submission to his heavenly Father's plan was everything. And you and I, who are his disciples, must be ready to take our orders, to toe the line, as he did.

After all, there is something to be said for cultivating the spirit of discipline, even among the laity. Just because the laws of the country are man-made laws, that is no reason why we should think it a fine thing to do, to break them. Take the single, obvious case of driving on the roads—that terrible total of accidents every month, which make peace-time as dangerous to life and limb as war-time was. Every now and then a fuss is made about it, and people write to the papers asking why we can't have wider roads, and forbid pedestrians to use them, why we can't have stronger brakes and larger road-signals and goodness knows what. The only thing they don't mention is that nearly everybody breaks the law some of the time, and a lot of people break the law most of the time, because they've no instinct of discipline. They always hope that this is the one corner or the one hump in the road that hasn't got a concealed car coming the other way, so they take risks and pass the people in front of them. Sometimes it is, sometimes it isn't.

And if laws are important, human conventions, the conventions of society, have their importance too. We say of some people, in tones of admiration, "He's so delightfully unconventional". Well, there are all sorts of ways of being unconventional; some better, some worse. So far as outward appearance and behaviour is concerned, I don't think the reputation of being unconventional is one which a priest ought to aim at. But that is all by the way; we are thinking not so much of the way in which human laws and conventions interfere with our liberty, as of the ecclesiastical obedience we owe, whether to the rules which the Church lays down for us, or to your superiors. What is our reaction to all that, after long years of enforced obedience in the seminary? What is it, and what ought it to be?

I don't think there can be any doubt that we carry away with us from the seminary the *habit* of discipline. We had the story at St. Edmund's, and I suppose you have the same story here, of the cabman passing in the road who waved his whip at the College and said "That's the priest-factory". And of course there *is* a certain amount of seminary training that works by mass-production; the mere drill. It's extraordinary to see how a lot of priests in choir at High Mass know instinctively when to get up and sit down and take their birettas off, all like one man, though you know some of them are really saying office all the time. But it goes deeper than drill; the newly-ordained priest is good at saying Yes, Father, and No, Father, and has learned to fetch and carry, and doesn't mind getting up at unconscionable hours in the morning. It is good for a man to carry the yoke in his youth; and the Catholic priesthood all over the world has, deservedly, the reputation of obeying orders. But mere obedience, though it's certainly a good thing, isn't everything. I can imagine our Lord saying, somehow, "Do not even the Communists the same?"

What you will not carry away with you from the seminary as a thing automatically produced, is the *spirit* of obedience. It is for *that* you must pray. It differs from the mere habit of obedience in three ways. It makes you ready to do the maximum, not the minimum, which your commission requires of you. It makes you ready to obey without murmuring, when the thing you have been ordered to do goes very much against the grain. And it makes you go on obeying orders when to do so is to risk great dangers, perhaps death. Let me just draw out, for a moment, the implications of that; only for a moment.

By God's mercy, you are going to be a priest. Don't forget that you are also going to be the junior curate somewhere. Because you are the junior curate, you will do all the least interesting jobs; the other curates will see to that. You will find yourself down to talk to the Children of Mary on Thursday evening; and you will be assured that anything will do for them. If you let anything do for the Children of Mary, by the time you are a rector you will be incapable of preaching a decent sermon. If you set about your ministry in a slave-minded way, everything will turn to slavery. No, when your rector tells you to preach to the Children of Mary, interpret that as an order to preach *well* to the Children of Mary. Give good measure from the start, and good measure will be poured into your bosom.

That first, then—interpret your instructions handsomely.

And next, let us hope your first curacy will be a great success. You and your rector will get on like a house on fire; you will be telling the bishop that you couldn't possibly be happier, he will be telling the bishop he had no idea they turned out such nice curates nowadays. Now, what is the temptation which comes to the bishop when *that* happens? I don't say he will succumb to it, but the temptation will be to say, "It seems rather a waste to have Father X working with such an easy-going rector as Canon Y. Let us give Canon Y that very difficult curate whom everybody finds such a nuisance; let us send Father X to that very exacting rector who can never keep a curate more than six months". And your dream will be over; your next curacy will be a time of probation, to test the metal you are made of. If you can accept the exchange without complaining about it, then there are some hopes of you. You have found the spirit of obedience.

And the third point—well, that is hardly worth developing. Thank God, the Church has a good record of heroism. The disciple is not above his Master; it may be, he wants you to be, like himself, *obediens usque ad mortem.*

# 11

# PERSEVERANCE

The hymns used in the Divine Office—I mean, the earlier ones, which were written by St. Ambrose or in the Ambrosian tradition—are perhaps deserving of more study than they usually get. They are not easy; Latin is used as an unwilling instrument to represent ideas deeper than it is qualified to express, and the thought of the writer is often bafflingly obscure. Yet it seems a pity that this early Christian poetry is skimmed over without reflection by us who say office, and is known to the laity hardly at all. I thought I would like to utilize one of them for the purposes of a retreat meditation; it is the hymn we say every day at None, *Rerum Deus tenax vigor.* The subject I want to talk about will come out as we go on; simplest, perhaps, to call it Perseverance.

The three hymns of terce, sext and none are obviously a sequence. They were not meant to be recited one after another in rapid succession about ten o'clock at night. They register three moods of the ordinary working day, assumed for the purposes of argument to be a fine day, and with no nonsense about Summer Time. There is the freshness of morning, there is the glaring heat of mid-day, there is the languid cool of early evening. And behind that, under the image of that, they register three moods of the full human life; the ardour of youth, the concentrated effort of middle life, the slackening off which comes with old age. Perhaps in the terce hymn the point is made less clear; that is because the Church can never forget that Pentecost happened about nine o'clock in the morning, and at nine o'clock in the morning, every day, she must invoke the Holy Spirit. But in the second verse you get down to the business of the day, *Flammescat igne caritas, Accendat ardor proximos;* "May our charity burst into flame, and set all around us on fire too". The ardour of youth; its eagerness to found societies and start new magazines and write round trying to get people to contribute; its impatience to make everybody see the world with its own eyes—something of that we ought to recapture, even the oldest of us, when we recite this hymn at terce.

When we get on to sext, we have to make allowances. We are so accustomed to living in a temperate climate, that we forget the conditions under which the Bible was written— and, for the matter of that, the conditions under which the breviary hymns were written. In Mediterranean countries, at any rate during the summer months, the mid-day sun is an enemy; you ask to be delivered from the pestilence that walks under the noon, you expect a special bonus if you have borne the burden and heat of the day. That is why our Lord says his heavenly Father "makes his sun rise on the evil and equally on the good, his rain fall on the just and equally on the unjust". Most people miss the order of the words; the point is that Almighty God makes his uncomfortable hot sun rise on the evil—yes, but equally on the good; lets his nice cool rain fall on the just—yes, but equally on the unjust. At sext, then, we pray to the God who controls all these vicissitudes of temperature, lights up the morning with brightness, and the noon with burning flames, and our prayer is *Aufer calorem noxium*, "take away the injurious heat". Three hours ago, we were praying for a conflagration, now we are beginning to think of the Minimax.

That all fits in, doesn't it? I mean, when you get down to it, the ardours of youth are all very well, but one doesn't want them to last a life-time; they are too tempestuous, too unregulated. Sooner or later a man has got to grow up, and see things as they are, and make allowances for other people's points of view; he has got to settle down mentally. Otherwise, he will be a perpetual focus of strain and conflict; that is why we pray *Extingue flammas litium*, "damp down the fires of quarrelsomeness"; he has got to learn to fit in. *Confer salutem corporum*, "grant us bodily health"—there, no doubt, the hymn is thinking of the hot noon and all its literal dangers. But when it goes on *Veramque pacem cordium*, "and true peace of mind", it is thinking of man's life, and the more temperate judgements which ought to come with middle age. No, not flabbiness, not readiness to compromise; "true peace", not just any kind of peace. A man must learn to possess his own soul before he really grows up.

So far terce and sext; and now we get on to the hymn I want to talk about, which is surely the best of the lot. *Rerum*

*Deus tenax vigor*—that line alone would be enough to make a meditation out of. "O God, the persistent sap of things"— no, don't tell me I'm being irreverent, don't tell me I'm using Pantheist language; that's what it says. And that's what we're wanting to say all the time, only it's so difficult to get our minds focussed on it, let alone find any way of expressing it. As the sap lends life to the tree, so God lends all things their existence. He is what gives reality its realness; if he did not exist, things just wouldn't be there. If you find the thought of God feeling remote from your mind, something abstract, something unsubstantial, you have only to go on your way repeating *Rerum Deus tenax vigor!* It is not just that he has created things; if God ceased to exist, creation wouldn't slowly fade out, like the ripples left behind by the stone you threw into the water. It just wouldn't be there.

*Immotus in te permanens,* "in thyself remaining ever unmoved"—while God is everything to his creation, his creation is, strictly speaking, nothing to him. He has a life of his own, altogether outside time, into which no echo of our earthly jarring can intrude. *Lucis diurnae tempora Successibus determinans;* he, the timeless, the unchangeable, maps out our existence, yours and mine, by that time-succession which is the measure of change. And each day is a working model, as it were, of that mysterious truth. The sun marks out the hours for us, casts the shadow that creeps over the dial, yet (as we know) the sun is not really moving; it is, as far as that is possible to a created and material thing, *immotus in se permanens.* No wonder, then, that as we see the sun verging towards the western horizon, we should be reminded of our own mortality; the thought of God's eternity casts over our brief lives the shadow of impermanence. At None, we must be thinking of old age; of how we pass, and God remains.

And our prayer, now, is *Largire lumen vespere*, "When evening comes, lavish thy light on us". It is a hackneyed thing to say, but there are compensations about the melancholy of a summer evening. To be sure, the sun has lost its strength, has become a spectacle to be contemplated, no longer an influence to be felt; a chill has crept into the air; the light is fading, and before long it will be impossible to read. And yet, as we know, the dying sun has reserved his best splendours for the last; not till now have we seen it making castles and bays out of the clouds that linger in the sky, not till now has so soft a glow, so delicate a gradation between light and shadow, picked out the beauties of earth. There is a calm about us, a coolness, a sense of completion, which we missed hitherto. A hundred poets and painters have immortalized the picture, but somehow it has not been staled for us; it is a fresh revelation every time. And will not old age, we ask, offer compensations of the same kind? Inevitable that a man's powers should decline; that there should be less enterprise about his decisions, less originality about his thought, less gift for making new friendships, and so on. But surely there will be a kind of mellow radiance about old age which will compensate us, if only in part, for what we have lost? Our passions will have cooled, the demands we make upon life will be fewer, we shall have gathered wisdom with the years; the experience of living may be less rich, but there will be a peace of mind, a calmness of view, which will help to compensate for all that. The sunshine of our days will have gained in splendour what it has lost in intensity.

That guess we might make, even if we were still heathens, comforting ourselves with the consolations of philosophy. But we are Christians, breathing the airs of grace; and surely to us it ought to seem more natural than ever, this idea of perfection in old age? We live with two lives simultaneously; and one of them, the natural life, is evidently destined to decline. The machinery of our bodies, like all machinery, wears itself out at last, and that has its effect even on the mind; our memories become weak, our attention is less capable of sustained effort, and so on. But the supernatural life which grace implants in us is not subject to these physical laws; all that is spiritual in us will survive the decline of our natural powers. May we not even suppose that it will shine out more clearly than ever in old age? As the shell of the natural wears thin, all the more visibly will the light of the supernatural shine out in us. And we have, most of us, before now met people—one or two people—in whom something of that kind seemed to have taken place; old age seemed to have eaten away their natural personalities, leaving nothing but grace. *Largire lumen vespere*, how attractive a thing, when you do see it, is that evening splendour of a Christian life! *Quo vita nusquam decidat*; "let there be no symptoms of decline"—so the hymn goes on to pray, and we can understand what it means. Symptoms of decline there must be in the physical order; hair and teeth and eyesight were not built for eternity. But in the spiritual order the life of any devout person will lead up to a *crescendo*, its last years will be its crowning years, ripe for heaven.

Forgive me if I ask, whether that is the impression you, personally, have got about very old people in general?

Don't think that I am trying to poke fun at anybody; I am much too far on the way myself to feel that it's a subject for amusement. But if you think of the ordinary Christians you know who are over eighty, quite good Christians, who have been going to the sacraments regularly for years and years, and obviously mean to save their souls, isn't there reason to fear that such people react in the wrong way, the unexpected way, to the near prospect of death? We expect them to be calm and peaceful; instead, they are crotchety, nervous, exacting, a constant burden on the patient relatives who have to look after them. Instead of being content to fade out of things and let their juniors have a chance, they are domineering in conversation, and insist on having an audience for jokes and anecdotes dating from their youth. Instead of taking a tolerant view about men and things, such as you would have expected their long experience to have bred in them, they are full of crusted prejudices, and voluble in their criticism of people they dislike. They are touchy and jealous of their privileges, just when you would think these toys meant nothing to them; they boast of past achievement, just when the thought of approaching judgement ought to humble them; they are greedy of their few remaining pleasures, just when they ought to be weaned away from the enjoyments of earth. *Quo vita nusquam decidat*, no symptom of decline! Isn't it quite common to find, in such people, that a whole world of imperfections have survived into old age, some discovered themselves with old age, some, perhaps, even developed in old age—symptoms of decline everywhere!

Please don't go away saying that I gave you a meditation only meant for people over eighty. That isn't at all the point of what I am trying to say. It is the hymn for None I am talking about, not the hymn for vespers, let alone the hymn for compline. None corresponds, surely, to the time of life at which we begin to feel that we are on the downward slope, without having yet—or so we like to think—got down very far. We are old enough to have begun watching, rather nervously, the habits of our seniors, wondering what it feels like to be like that. We notice traits, foibles, crotchets in them, which surprise and alarm us. Surprise us, because they don't fit in with the picture we have formed of old age as a kind of mellow sunset. Alarm us, because, when we come to think of it, aren't we getting just the tiniest bit like that ourselves? Don't we find ourselves reluctant to be helped into our great-coats? That reluctance is the first sign of old age. Then it is that we ought to recite this hymn at none with particular devotion, saying to ourselves, "This means me". *Sed praemium mortis sacrae perennis instet gloria*; yes, by all means let us pray for the grace of a holy death. But that shouldn't be all. Let us pray also for the grace to avoid, and to fight down, those imperfections which so often mar old age, looking out for them and meeting them and resisting them as they come. That, surely, is involved in the notion of perseverance.

To be sure, in its ordinary theological connotation perseverance means being in a state of grace when death overtakes us, that and nothing more. But perseverance, like faith,

like charity, can mean so much more than its ordinary theological use would imply. It can mean, not merely staying the
course, but winning a race; not merely refusing to drop out,
but finishing (if I may put it vulgarly—I don't think St. Paul
would have minded the phrase) finishing with a sprint. To
be always trying to go forward, and not merely stand still,
that, surely, is the first sign of being in the right way. You
feel so much happier, sometimes, about people who are
fighting a desperate battle against fierce and ignominious
temptations, than about people who just jog along, clear of
mortal sin, and seem quite happy about it. The *Imitation of
Christ*, that bouquet of brambles which the piety of the later
Middle Ages has left to us, gives us a nasty dig in the meditation on death. "Here you go" it says, "praying for a long
life, when for all you know a long life will be full of danger
for you". The reference, I suppose, is to mortal sins; but I
think we can apply the same consideration to our Purgatory.
Is it really much use to us draining the lees of life, if our old
age is to be disfigured by all these imperfections, this all-
round deciduousness which is so exactly the opposite of
what the hymn tells us to pray for?

The none-tide of life, when we are beginning to feel the
advance of the years, has perhaps no more subtle danger
than the temptation to mark time, instead of going forward.
A certain exhaustion has fallen even on our mental powers,
and effort is, more than ever, distasteful to us. We have got
accustomed to our own low standard of achievement; the
very humility with which we confess our past faults brings
with it a kind of despair; we are only second-class articles,
after all. We have even, perhaps, without quite realizing it,

grown somewhat cynical about the possibilities of human nature as a whole; we have seen so much falling-away, so much falling-off, in the lives of our neighbours. Favourite authors, favourite prayers, favourite subjects of meditation have lost their appeal; use has staled them for us. I sometimes wish that Holy Church, in her great resourcefulness, could dig out for us and canonize some Saint who only started to serve God when he was about sixty. I don't know of one; even St. Thomas of Canterbury was only forty-two when he started, and he was a martyr. Yet it must be possible, or how did those labourers in the vineyard who came in at None or even later get the same wages as the people who set to work when the bell rang for terce? It would be a comfort to have just one!

At least let us do this, let us watch our habits. Those habits especially which grow upon one, habit-forming habits. I mean, for example, lying rather longer in bed, because we are not quite as young as we were. I mean such things as monopolizing the conversation; that becomes easier and easier to do as we acquire more and more seniority, and incidentally as we become a bit deaf. And again, complaining about things; as we grow older and older we shall have more and more to complain about, and therefore if we can manage to complain less about the things which we have to complain about, we shall strike a fair average. And again, depressing other people, particularly our juniors, with long diatribes about how the world is going from bad to worse; that is a special temptation of old age, because we like to console ourselves with the thought that the world we shall soon leave is a world not worth living in. It doesn't do any harm to *think* that, but it is extraordinary what a blight you can cast over your immediate neighbourhood by constantly saying that. All those things grow on one, and without one's noticing it, that's the trouble. As I say, we can do something to detect our own bad habits by watching our criticisms of other people, whether in books or in real life. I don't mean we should watch other people on purpose to pick holes in them; but if you do find yourself registering a ciriticism of anybody a bit older than yourself, don't fail to reflect, "Let me see, am I like that?"

*Quo vita nusquam decidat*—much must needs decline; our bodily powers, our mental alertness, our appreciation of the savours of life. But, in so far as we refuse to be got down by all that, there will be no decline, and the clouds that gather round our sunset will be tinged with gold.

# 12

## CONFERENCE ON PRAYER

I want to give you a sort of meditation, or perhaps I should rather call it a sort of conference, about prayer. But please let me do it on the understanding that I am not laying down the law; I am simply contributing a few suggestions for your common consideration. I would as willingly hear what anybody else has to say, as say this myself. Partly because I don't feel any special claim to speak on the subject, and partly because the subject itself is one on which Holy Church leaves us so free to differ in our opinions. It's an extraordinary thing, when you come to think of what prayer is (or ought to be) to us priests, the atmosphere in which we live and the thing we are paid to do, that there is no thesis about prayer in the dogmatic theology we do in the seminary. I think the reason is that you really can't lay down the law; the whole subject is full of paradox. And for the most part, I shall be simply putting before you a series of dilemmas, and indicating my own solution of them, without even hinting that my solution is the right one; let each abound in his own sense. I would speak first of all about prayer in the narrow sense, *rogatio*, asking God for favours. Then I would speak about prayer in the broad sense, *oratio*, talking to God. And then I would say something about distractions, and what we can do, the very little we can do, to avoid or overcome distractions when we pray.

First of all, about asking for temporal blessings which we want for ourselves. Our Lord has taught us to pray, "Give us this day tomorrow's bread". We haven't time to discuss Greek, but I think that is clearly what the words mean; we are not just asking for something on the table, we are asking for something in the larder. On the other hand, he has told us, "Take no thought for the morrow, what you shall eat, for your Heavenly Father knoweth that you have need of all these things". I don't find that a difficult dilemma to solve. I think he means that we *should* ask him for temporal favours, and even (what we generally forget to do) ask him for things which seem to come as a matter of course, like the baker's van. (Bakers' vans don't come as a matter of course all over Europe.) But at the same time he warns us to ask for the simple things, the necessities of life, not the luxuries. And he warns us not to look too far ahead; tomorrow is far enough. The remote future, what might happen to us, for good or evil, is best left in his hands with a general act of resignation to his will.

And then, about asking for what we want for other people. Here I don't think it is very important to distinguish between temporal and spiritual blessings, because after all there is nothing selfish about wanting our friends to be happy and comfortable even in this world. The difficulty here is, to my own mind, When somebody says "Pray for me, won't you?", and we say, "Yes," what exactly are we committed to? (I think I've read somewhere, but I may have dreamt it, that St. Francis of Assisi, on such occasions, used to kneel down at once and say the prayer he was asked for, to get it off his chest, so to speak. There was nothing St. Francis hated so much as taking thought for the morrow.) How much does charity bind us to go on thinking about all our friends, and all their needs? And there are a great many people who need our prayers, and don't ask us to pray for them. Put the dilemma in this way, if you like. If we were really unselfish, shouldn't we spend the whole of our available spare time in saying Hail Mary's for other people? And on the other hand, if we did do that, wouldn't our prayer remain on a rather mechanical level, and could we ever hope to advance in the ways of the Spirit?

All I would like to suggest there is a rough, practical solution. Avoid (I would say) the kind of scruple which will interfere with your liberty of spirit. Don't get your prayers cluttered up with a long litany of names which cease to have any meaning for you because you have repeated it so often. Don't ransack your brains, in your times of prayer, to make sure that you haven't left out some of the people you ought to be praying for. Don't dwell on the thought of the people you are praying for, imagining to yourself the dangers they are in or the discomforts they are suffering; that is waste of time. Just remind yourself of the names you want to remember, and in doing so remind yourself that they are only types of millions and millions of other people in the world whose needs you would be worrying about if you knew them better.

Then fold them all up in an envelope, so to speak, and enclose them in your prayers, the prayers you are just going to say; it may be the Mass, or your office, or your private devotions, but obviously the Mass is best. If they recur to your mind at all in the course of your prayer, think about them for a moment but don't dwell on them. Let them be the undertones of your commerce with God.

And then there's praying for spiritual favours for oneself. That at least, you would imagine, ought to be fairly plain sailing. Well, I don't want to upset anybody's peace of mind; but the more I read the spiritual authors, the more clearly is it borne in on me that there are two distinct types of Catholic piety which approach this subject in entirely opposite ways. There is a piety which is so humble that it is asking for all kinds of spiritual favours all the time. And there is the piety which is so generous that it won't ask for any spiritual favours, except perhaps the gift of final perseverance; I want God (it says), not God's gifts—or, still more boldly, I don't want to get anything out of my prayer, I want it to be all giving. When a soul is sufficiently advanced in the ways of the Spirit to realize what a lot of things it needs, it has become so disinterested in its love of God that it no longer wants to ask for them.

· How are we going to resolve this dilemma? Why, I think the simplest thing to say is that it doesn't very much matter which kind of prayer we make; and that it is perfectly possible for the same soul to pray now in one way, now in another. If we get into the habit of following our instincts in the matter of prayer—which is certainly the right thing to do, because they are not really instincts, they are God's invitations to the soul—then on the one hand we shall not be shy about asking great things of God; heroic love, if you will, martyrdom if you will. Only we should never, I think, ask for spiritual consolations; those are God's treats, and it is bad manners to ask for treats. And we should not gratify our imaginations, or frighten them, by picturing to ourselves minutely all the sacrifices God might call on us to make, all the sanctity he might see fit to bestow on us; that is wasting time. On the other hand, if we feel moved to pray with St. Ignatius, "Give me only thy love and thy grace, and I am rich enough, I ask for nothing more", then I think God will be equally ready to accept that form of prayer, and will not let us be the losers by it.

Well, now let's go on to prayer in its more general sense; not simply asking for things, but doing our best to cultivate (if that isn't too presumptuous a word) the presence of God in our souls. And there is one difficulty about that which naturally occurs to all of us. The apostle tells us to pray without ceasing; but we have all of us got our work to do, and charity makes certain calls upon us, and we must even have a certain amount of time for relaxation if we are to keep fresh; how are we going to work all that in, without ceasing to pray? I can't do two things at once; and yet at nearly every moment of the day I have two simultaneous duties; I have to be praying and I have to be getting on with my job. There's the dilemma.

Well, of course it isn't strictly true that it is impossible to do two things at once. Holy people have, before now, managed to keep the presence of God continually before their minds when they were engaged in the most distracting occupations. I think it was Marie de l'Incarnation who had to do the business accounts for a firm which was run by her family, and went on praying all the time; though she admitted that she was glad of dipping her pen in the ink sometimes, because one could think harder about God while one was doing that. Still, we know that that is beyond our standard. Let us think first about our fixed times of prayer, and then whether we can't make some distant, faltering attempt in our own lives to realize the ideal of prayer at all times.

Every priest ought to have a meditation time in his orders for the day. Not necessarily before Mass; that is, for many of us, a time when we can't reckon on having any leisure. Later in the day will do; and if anything interferes, still later in the day. Only don't try to make it last thing at night; if you haven't made it by the time you take your last meal, tell God you wish you had been able to manage it, and leave it at that. A visit to the Blessed Sacrament some time in the course of the evening is worth thinking about, too, even if it only works out at ten minutes or so. Have some time when you are at leisure to be with God, apart from the prayers which are binding on you by obligation. And at the same time, try to practise recalling God to your memory at odd times of the day. Some people can make ejaculatory prayers, and mean them; I can't. Some people can make a deliberate act of love to God whenever they hear the clock strike, without getting into mechanical habits about it; I can't. What I would suggest is that now and again, when you think of it, you should let your mind fall back upon God in between your other occupations, just for a moment; when you are reaching out for a cigarette, or when you are waiting for a 'bus. Don't try to say prayers, exactly; just let your mind rest on the thought of God. And if at any time you feel yourself particularly pleased with life, let your mind fall back upon God and share your happiness with him. Habits like that will be a sort of ground-work for a more constant sense of God's presence.

And here's the next problem to decide; what kind of mental prayer ought we to go in for? The kind that comes easiest to us, or the kind that comes most difficult? If we always use the prayer that comes easiest to us, what is it but a form of self-indulgence? If we use the prayer that goes against the grain, aren't we presumptuously depending on our own effort, instead of leaving everything to God's grace? Ought we always to be pumping up acts of the will, as if everything depended on our own agency? Or ought we to let our hearts rest lovingly on God, and be accused of self-pleasing? Mental prayer seems to be either a form of pride, or a form of idleness.

I don't think there's any difficulty at all in solving that dilemma, as a matter of principle. Do whatever God's invitation calls you to do. If you find it natural to use your own effort, don't be afraid that you are resisting grace. Grace and human effort aren't two separate forces, at work side by side; it is grace that makes in you the effort which you make. If God seems to call you to a more restful form of prayer, and your confessor does not forbid you the use of it, make that your form of prayer, not stopping to worry about self-pleasing. Prayer isn't self-torture; it is talking to God.

But another objection to mental prayer is possible. What exactly is it meant to do? Is it meant to train our imaginations, our affections, and our wills by putting them, as it were, through a course of gymnastics? That is the impression our reading sometimes gives us; but if so, we ask, is that really prayer at all? Isn't it, at best, a kind of self-cultivation? Or is mental prayer simply a way of doing honour to God? And if that is all, would not it be safer to go on saying prayers, reciting the rosary or going round the stations, so as to make sure we were doing something, not just idling? We have been using mental prayer for years, and it doesn't seem to have made much difference to our characters; have we any reason to think that this form of worship is specially pleasing to God?

To that objection, I have only a word to say, which I will leave with you; I may be quite wrong. I think mental prayer is imperative, if only to plough up the mind and leave it fallow for God's inspirations. He may want to tell you about something you are meant to do for him; and, although he does not need our help in creating the opportunity for him, it seems to me that we are wrong if we do not create it. All the Masses and all the office we say can leave his voice unheard; we shout it down with our importunities.

And now it is time we said something about distractions in prayer. The first difficulty here is, I suppose, What is the good of my talking to you about distractions in prayer? Either they are voluntary, in which case there is no advice to be given except, Stop them; or they are involuntary, in which case no advice can be of any use. Well, of course the dilemma there is only an apparent one. Let us get rid of a great deal of unreal talk about voluntary distractions. Oh, I know the Catechism tells us that those who think neither of

God nor of what they say are offending God; a sentence which has done infinite harm. It may be good theology, but it isn't real life. The distractions we are really concerned to avoid aren't voluntary; they are only semi-voluntary—venial sins at the worst, and for the most part only imperfections. And we can do something—not much, but something—to avoid them. Don't choose a room where the wireless is on when you say your office. Don't, if you can help it, say your office late at night, when you are tired. Don't try to squeeze it in at odd moments just before the next meal, so that you will be in a hurry. Find out which makes you less distracted, saying it all in a lump or spacing it out, and vary your practice accordingly. (Very few priests seem to think of saying only one of the day hours at a time; but that is what the day hours were meant for.) Don't artificially create strong interests in your life which will buzz in your head during your times of prayer. And, as I was trying to say earlier on, try to cultivate the habit of letting your mind go back to God and rest on him at odd moments during the day. That will give you more chance of finding yourself recollected when you come to perform the opus Dei. If you are honest with yourself in observing one or two rules like that (another one, by the way; don't do odd jobs like opening the window or stoking the fire while you are saying office), it will be safe to assume that the distractions which still remain are INvoluntary. Distractions at Mass nearly always are.

And another dilemma meets you when you are told in pious books that you ought to fight against your distractions. How can I fight against them (you very reasonably ask) and go on saying office all the time—still more go on saying Mass all the time? The fight against distractions is a distraction in itself. Hard enough for the men who rebuilt Jerusalem under Nehemias, to work with trowels in their hands and swords ready at their sides for fear of hostile attack; it would have been worse if they had had to carry a sword and a trowel in the same hand, and that is what I'm expected to do! Personally, I think that dilemma is a perfectly genuine one, and on the whole people should not be encouraged to fight against distractions, if that phrase has any meaning. Or rather, let me distinguish. I think many of us find that there are times in our prayer when everything is going swimmingly; when our attention is caught up to God, without any special effort of our own, when a warm glow of devotion seems to animate us, unaccountably, while we pray. Even at these times, distractions may come to us; and at these times we may (I don't say exactly fight against them, but) brush them aside without much difficulty, like Abraham fending off the birds that would have come and eaten up his burnt sacrifice. Quite gently, not arguing with them; simply saying to yourself, "Not now; some other time will do to think about that".

But I'm only recommending this when our prayer is at its best. When it's on a more ordinary level, and you are hard put to it to keep yourself in God's presence at all, to fight against your distractions is like trying to fight against a wasp which is buzzing round you; for some reason, the beast seems only the more anxious to settle down. No, when you come to yourself and find that your attention has been wandering, perhaps for a whole nocturn together, simply put your nose down into the book again and try to recollect yourself. Don't even make an act of contrition about it, just then, leave that till you say the *Sacrosanctae* after compline. One other hint I would give you for what it is worth; if you find that you are fidgeting, kicking a leg or drumming with your fingers on your knee, Stop fidgeting. For some reason, recollection is easier, I think, when you are keeping quite still.

And now for a last dilemma. If I find that my prayer is, or know that my prayer is going to be, a mass of distractions, though they be involuntary ones, is it worth while trying to pray at all? (I'm thinking of prayers which are not of obligation now.) Wouldn't it be better to do some spiritual reading or even go out and do some visiting instead? Because you have told me that prayer is thinking about God, and if I'm not thinking about God, I don't see how I am to describe myself as praying. Here I would return a decided answer; Never give in like that. Go through the motions of praying, if that is all you can do, and when you have finished, offer it up to God in a spirit of great humility. Tell him he knows your fashioning, knows you are but dust; deplore the natural weakness which makes it so hard for you, his creature, to do the thing you were put into the world to do. Confess to him, at the same time, the habitual want of seriousness and purpose in your life which prevents you attaining recollection when you want it. Tell him you wish your prayer had been one long peaceful aspiration to him; unite it with the prayer of our Blessed Lord while he was on earth, and ask to have it accepted with that mantle cast over it. Offer to God your will, the will that is so weak, and has achieved so little. Then perhaps (who knows?) this distracted prayer of yours may be more acceptable to God than the most fervent prayer you ever offered in your life. He wants us to throw ourselves at his feet; he does not need to be told that we are sinners.

I think that when our account comes to be audited at the Judgement, the record of the prayers we said will be a surprise for most of us, and, for very many of us, the surprise will not be a disappointment.

# 13

# OUR LADY

I have to talk to you about our Blessed Lady. I hope you will excuse me if I do not give you a theological statement about our Lady's position, and her privileges. For some reason, if there is one supposedly English word which annoys me and depresses me, it is "Mariology". Some other preacher, no doubt, might give you a strictly theological discourse on the subject, and send you away with awakened minds, and full hearts. If I made the attempt, my efforts would present, I know, the character of dried seaweed. No, we will have no Mariology. We are just going to talk about our Blessed Lady.

Only, by way of putting our thoughts into some kind of shape, we will tackle the subject on the lines of history. Every human being exists, in a sense, from eternity to eternity. From eternity, you and I existed in the mind of God. But we existed only as a thought in his mind; the actual world got on well enough without us, and, until the last few negligible moments, our entry into it was neither expected nor desired. Then, for a few brief years, the light of actuality caught us, like the shadow of a stranger passing your window-blind. This was our "life"; these years were given us to cut a figure of some sort in the world, and leave a memory behind us. That memory is short and fading; even the fame of great men in the past, although it lingers, becomes distant and unreal; loses its clearness of outline. I just want to point out that our Lady's history is the exact opposite of all that. Her presence in the world was expected and desired, by all those chosen souls who shared God's counsels, ever since the moment when Adam and Eve lost their Paradise. When she came to us, it was her first preoccupation to cut no figure in the world at all. And since she left it, the memory of her has become closer to us and more real to us than ever; its outlines have actually become clearer to us with the lapse of time.

The ancient Greek dramatists, as we know, took their stories from a common stock of familiar legends, so that the audience always knew, from the start, how the play was going to end. You missed, therefore, something of the thrill which the modern play-goer expects. But, in revenge, you had the comfortable feeling of being in the know, when the characters on the stage, supposedly, were not. This gave rise to the enjoyment of "tragic irony", when some character on the stage "spoke truer than he meant to"—used language which became more appropriate if you knew, as the audience did and the actors didn't, the ins and outs of the story; knew, for example, that Jocasta was Oedipus' mother when Oedipus only thought of her as his wife. And I think a Christian, reading the Old Testament, has something of the same advantage. He knows the end of the story; and consequently all the events, and even sometimes the language, of the Old Testament, will have a new meaning for him.

I don't know what it would be like reading the Old Testament if you were an orthodox Jew; that's different. But if you imagine yourself as a crass atheist reading through the Old Testament, I think you would find that it has its *longueurs*. It is, after a fashion, the history of a people; but it is very untidily told, with long gaps, and a disproportionate emphasis on a few leading ideas. But if you read it as a Christian the whole thing comes to life. The story of it begins with the Fall, and the prophecy that the seed of the woman will be at war with the serpent, crushing his head; we realize that that is the promise of a redemption. And the drama of the Old Testament is that this redemption is continually just going to come off, but never does. The climax is still there awaiting us, when we turn over the page from the Old Testament into the New.

And we know that the end of the story, like the beginning of it, is to have a heroine as well as a hero. Almighty God has been represented as saying to the serpent, not, as we should expect, "I will put enmity between thee and the man", but "I will put enmity between thee and the woman, and . . . her seed". What we are on the look-out for, then, all through the Old Testament, what keeps us on our toes all the time, is looking for a *woman* who will come up to the required specifications; the woman whose obedience will reconnect that link between the human and the divine, which Eve's disobedience has fatally severed. Here, for instance, is Sara, the wife of Abraham; long past the age of

child-bearing. Angelic visitors announce that she is to have
a son; and Sara, at the back of the tent, laughs. *She* won't
do; she laughs. Isn't it tantalizing, the way that situation
recurs, the situation we are all waiting for, when an angel
appears to announce the birth of a son? First to Sara, before
Isaac is born; and then to the wife of Manue, before Samson
is born; and then, but this time to his father, St. Zachary,
before John the Baptist is born; and always it is an anti-
climax. Isaac is the child of promise, but the promises are
not fulfilled in him; Samson is the deliverer of his people,
but only from the Philistines; and John the Baptist is not the
Light, he only comes to bear witness of the Light. A series
of announcements, but the Annunciation has not come
yet. . . .

All through the Old Testament you get that curious feeling of having come across this situation before; and then you
remember that it's not quite like that—you are going to
come across it later on, when you reach the gospels. All that
enormous preoccupation with the survival of king David's
succession; when Bersabee comes to David in his old age,
and claims the right of her son Solomon to succeed; or when
Athalia kills all the princes of the blood royal except one,
Joas, who is saved by his aunt Josaba—what does that remind you of? Yes, the massacre of the Innocents. The only
importance of all this, really, is that the kings of Juda were
our Lord's ancestors; if Joas hadn't been saved, our Lady
would never have been born. Bersabee is actually mentioned
in the list of our Lord's ancestors; so is Rahab, the woman
who was responsible for the fall of Jericho—the one weak
spot there, just as our Lady was the one weak spot in Satan's

domination of the world. So is Ruth, claimed in marriage by her kinsman.

And it's not only among the ancestresses of the Holy Family that you find coming events cast their shadows before them. Look at the other women of the Old Testament; neither Jael nor Judith quite comes up to our ideal of womanhood, and yet, because of what they stood for, the deliverance of their people, both Jael and Judith are hailed as "blessed among women". Esther, again, delivered her people, by interceding with the great king, as only she—he tells us so himself—had a right to intercede. Even in its most blood-thirsty passages, the Old Testament is always recalling these gracious memories to us, as when we watch Respha, the daughter of Aia, weeping over her sons that were crucified. It is the art of Virgil that, all through the *Aeneid*, he strikes a chord of mystery by prophecies and hints of things yet to come. You get the same impression in the Old Testament; but the Old Testament is not art.

There is a well-known passage in the Proverbs, where the Divine Wisdom is represented as assisting in the work of creation; "I was at his side, a master workman, my delight increasing with each day, as I made play before him all the while; made play in this world of dust, with the sons of Adam for my play-fellows". This audacious passage has been utilized by the liturgy for recitation on certain of our Lady's feasts. And I like to think of her as the world's play-fellow; a slight, girlish figure, appearing and disappearing all through those long centuries when the world was without hope; playing hide-and-seek with us till the time came. All the women of the Old Testament seem, if I may put it in that way with-

out irreverence, only imperfect studies which the artist has
executed, and then put on one side. Anna, for example, the
mother of Samuel, how like the Magnificat, in some ways,
is her song of triumph! And yet, how it falls short of the
Magnificat! A preliminary draft, which wouldn't do.

She came, so long expected, so long desired; you do not
introduce the heroine in the first scene of the drama. And
when she came, did she occupy the stage, did she take the
lime-light? She, the lime-light? Saints and theologians have
pored over the gospels, picking up every trace of her, like
men hoarding the relics of spilt treasure; how narrow is their
field of search! And notice that the moment her Son is born,
she appears only in connexion with him, only as subordinated
to him. "Going into the dwelling, they found the child there,
with his mother Mary"; and after that, she is not even mentioned by name. "Take with thee the child and his mother";
"the father and mother of the child were still wondering
over all that was said of him"—see how she has become
anonymous, even when he is lying in her arms. And when
she finds him in the temple, what does she say? "Think,
what anguish of mind thy father and I have endured." "Thy
father and I"—it sounds natural to us; but can you quote me
another sentence in the Bible, another sentence uttered in
antiquity, in which the speaker does not come first? "Shall
I and thy mother bow down to thee?"—so speaks the uxori-
ous Jacob. "Or I only and Barnabas"—so speaks the infinite
courtesy of St. Paul. But our Lady has more than good
manners, she has utter humility; Joseph's grief comes first,
because it matters most. All those years of her girlhood,
what is left of them? Only a few legends. All those months

when she followed her Son on his travels, and what can we glean from them? Only a few references, something less than gracious. Then, for a moment, she appears on Calvary; then, for a moment, she lights up the Cenacle. And the rest is silence; no word of her life, or even of her death; she has left us without a trace, without a tomb.

Such was her life; and since then, what has her fame been? On the whole, it has left very little mark on the earliest Christian literature. That, as we have seen, she came to undo what Eve did, was obvious from the first. You can trace the idea, I think, in St. Paul; St. Paul was very Fall-minded. "It was Adam" he writes, "who was created first, and Eve later; nor was it Adam that went astray; woman was led astray, and was involved in transgression. Yet woman will find her salvation in the Child-bearing"—that is, in our Lady's Child-bearing; no other interpretation gives any sense to the passage. I suspect that we ought to interpret another obscure saying of St. Paul's in the same way; "if woman takes her origin from man, man equally comes to birth through woman"—so he writes to the Corinthians. Did he merely mean that every woman has a father, and every man has a mother? Scarcely worth saying; besides, men have fathers, and women have mothers. Much more probably he is reminding us that if Eve came to us through Adam, the Second Adam came to us through the Second Eve. St. Irenaeus, in the second century, draws out the parallel explicitly. But texts like these come to us only as occasional confidences, they were not, it would seem, the commonplaces of Christian thought.

What are we to conclude? That the Christians of the first

age thought exactly as we do, felt exactly as we do, about the
Blessed Virgin, but for some reason—reverence, perhaps—
made little public allusion to her? I suppose that was, a
hundred years ago, the explanation which found most favour; even Newman's doctrine of development was suspect
in his day. But I think it is now more generally recognized
that there has been a progressive unfolding of Catholic theology, on this as on other subjects. If you compare the
decree which defined the Immaculate Conception with that
which defines the Assumption, I think you will notice that
whereas Pius IX is concerned to emphasize the unchang-
ing deposit of faith, Pius XII rather points us to a growing
conviction, as the centuries went on, about subjects which
had at first been a matter of hesitation. The Church has
made up her mind.

Clearly, the great Christological heresies of the fourth and
fifth centuries did much to concentrate attention on our
Lady as the hinge, without which our view of the hypostatic
union can get no leverage. If our Lord was born, not merely
from her, but of her, then he was truly Man. If he was at the
same time truly God, then she was, and must be called, the
Mother of God. Hence her new title of Theotokos; she becomes a theological symbol of the utmost importance, and
she takes the highest possible rank accordingly. In the litur-
gies of East and West alike she is celebrated in sonorous
phrases, and from the half-dome of the basilica her dark icon
looks down, challenging our faith. The orators, too, begin to
spread themselves, and by the seventh and eighth centuries
they have become as diffuse and tedious about our Blessed
Lady as any modern preacher. By the time of Charlemagne,

at latest, I think you can say that our Lady was honoured as widely, as publicly, as explicitly as she is to-day.

As much honoured, yes, but was she as much loved? It was left for the Middle Ages to teach us that. How on earth the Middle Ages, with all their barbarity, produced the whole notion of romantic love—of woman as something set apart, sacred, to be deserved, if she could be deserved at all, only by knightly devotion—is something I could never understand. But there it is; there are Dante and Beatrice, there are the troubadours; nobody disputes the fact. And nobody, I think, doubts that it was all bound up with a new attitude towards the person of our Blessed Lady; a spirit of knightly devotion which had grown up towards her. Writers as anti-Catholic as Comte and Lecky assure us that all our modern ideas about the dignity of womanhood come down to us from the opinion men had of our Blessed Lady in the Middle Ages. After all, why do we call her "our Lady"? It's not an official title; at least, only in the Church of England. If you look at the official calendar of the Church of England you will find the 25th of next month put down as the Annunciation of our Lady; but we call it by its old name, the Annunciation of the Blessed Virgin. The Reformers took over, instinctively, the pet name for her (as it were) to which Europe had grown accustomed; she was our Lady, we were her knights—the thing was as simple as that.

I should dearly like to go on about the Counter-Reformation and the centuries which followed it, but we haven't time. What about the history of the last hundred years? Most people outside the Church would say that in the course of a hundred years the Holy See has compelled the faithful to proclaim, on pain of heresy, the doctrine of our Lady's Immaculate Conception, and the doctrine of her bodily Assumption into heaven. Personally I think it would be nearer the truth, though of course not quite true, to say that the faithful have compelled the Holy See to proclaim those two doctrines. Compelled it to do so, I mean, by the unanimity of their faith in, and the warmth of their devotion to, the two doctrines in question, while they still remained undefined.

And the fact behind that is surely a deeper sense among the faithful at large about the unique dignity of the Blessed Virgin, and of the privileges which are likely to have been hers. If you are criticizing the Church from a detached point of view, from the outside, you explain that as you will. But if you have the faith, you are almost compelled to admit the principle I suggested at the beginning of this conference, that the fame of our Blessed Lady is destined by Providence to grow, not to dwindle, with the years; hers was never the common lot. Let us not conceal it, the effect of all this is a great deal of publicity; and modern publicity is often marred by vulgarity and hysteria. We shall not, all of us, like all the pieties and the bondieuseries which go with our Lady's cult. But underneath it, there is something deeper at work. I think she is, in a sense, closer to us nowadays than she was to earlier generations of Christians. She is something more to us than a theological symbol; nor do we think of her, in the manner of the Middle Ages, as the patroness of this or that institution, a religious order, or a parish, or a guild.

Rather, to each of us, she is a personal romance. Because a natural instinct makes us unwilling to discuss such things in public, I will leave it at that. The real secret of her influence on our lives is something undefined, something indefinable.

# 14

## FATHER *AND* MOTHER

King Solomon, the peaceful successor of the warlike king David, is the type in many ways of our Blessed Lord. And much has been handed down to us in connexion with his name which has reminded the Church, with her keen eye for mystical coincidence, of our Blessed Lady. Most of the Scripture lessons we recite on our Lady's feasts are taken from the books which belong to King Solomon's tradition. I want to speak now of our Blessed Lady; but I want to take as my starting-point a story of King Solomon's court which is not usually connected with the thought of her.

We all know the story of the two women who came before the king with a dispute about the identity of their children. Both lived in the same house, each had a child; one of the children died in the night, and it was not clear, next morning, whether the dead child had not been substituted for the living one. King Solomon, called upon to decide which was the true mother, ordered that the living child should be cut in half, and a half given to each. Obviously, it was only a gesture; as a solution of the difficulty it would have been, not only cruel, but ineffective. The gesture, however, was enough; one woman was prepared to accept the award, the other rejected it, even if it should mean losing the custody of the child. And the king had no hesitation in proclaiming that she, the woman who would not have the child murdered, was its true mother.

One detail about the story I think we are apt to miss. Why did the rival claimant welcome the suggestion that the child should be cut in two? There was a dead child already, and it was hers; why could not she be content with that? The answer, I think, is that the woman's acceptance of the award was a gesture, no less than the award itself. She didn't want the murder to happen; didn't think that the murder would happen. She fancied that she would be identified as the true mother, if she expressed herself content to receive half her rights, rather than nothing. A true mother (so she will have argued in her own mind) is above all things possessive about her child; alive or dead, it must be hers, her property. And if I insist on my claim to half the body, the king will take it for granted that the child is mine, and will hand it over to me, still living. Of course she was wrong. The true mother, obeying an instinct rather than a calculation, knew better; she knew that motherhood, real motherhood, is not possessive; its genius is just the opposite. A real mother does not want the child to belong to her; she wants to belong to the child. Though she should die in giving birth to it, or in defending it against attack, she wants the child to live; her life, her being has passed into it; she will live only in and for the life that has sprung from her. Let the child live, at all costs;

even though she, the true mother, should never fondle it in her arms and listen to its cries and watch its smile again.

This instinct of maternity has never been verified as it was verified in our Blessed Lady. No mother has ever lived for her child as she did. From the moment of the Nativity, she is content to recede into the background; to let our Lord live his own life, fulfil his own destiny, without a shadow of selfish interference on her part. She does not always understand why the sacrifice of her own feelings is necessary; "Son, why hast thou dealt thus with us? Thy father and I have sought thee in sorrow". But she is content with the answer, that he must be about his heavenly Father's business; she treasures up the saying and makes conjecture of its significance in her heart. The Heart of Mary—we recognize its purity, its tenderness; do we always recognize its considerateness, its willingness to let our Lord go his own way? When she stood on Calvary, her offering, like his, was complete; but her offering, like his, did not date from that moment; it was a life-long renunciation. For three years he gave himself; for all those three years she gave him—relinquished her own claim upon him, which would have bidden her dissuade him from the course he took; let him fulfil the destiny his heavenly Father had appointed for him.

We priests have a special claim, in more ways than one, to the patronage of our Blessed Lady. Our hands are privileged to touch his Eucharistic Body as hers were to hold and tend his natural Body. When we consecrate, he is born anew by a kind of sacramental birth; when we offer the bloodless sacrifice of the Mass, we associate ourselves with it as she associated herself with the sacrifice of Calvary. But I wonder whether we give as much thought as we might to a different side of the same truth; namely that she ought to be our model not only in our relation to the divine Mysteries, but in our relation to our spiritual children as well. For fear that the language I am going to use may seem strange and unhallowed by tradition, let me call your attention to the fact that our Lord expects his priests to exercise a motherly care over the faithful. He has told us that whosoever does the will of his Father in heaven becomes thereby his brother, his sister, and his mother. And St. Gregory, you will remember, interprets that phrase for us in one of the third nocturns. He says that you may become as it were the mother of Christ by preaching to others, and so bringing Christ to birth in their hearts. And St. Paul makes that claim especially for those engaged in apostolic work. "My little children"—so he writes to the Galatians—"with whom I am in labour afresh, until Christ be formed in you". By preaching to them and converting them he has already shewn himself a mother; and now, working and praying for their perfection, he is undergoing the pangs of motherhood afresh; he cannot be satisfied until Christ be fully formed in them.

I say, then, it is good Christian doctrine that the priest ought to be the mother as well as the father of his parish. His labours for men's souls make him, from one point of view, their father in Christ; make him, from another point of view, Christ's mother in them. Are we to say that that is an unreal distinction; or at any rate that it has only a mystical, not a practical importance? I don't think so. There is a difference, after all, in our common experience between a father's and a mother's love. The father, however great be his attach-

ment to his son, cannot help thinking of the son as a continuation or a repetition of himself. If the father's influence
is allowed to have its way, the eldest son is called by the
same name, is sent to the same school, is apprenticed to the
same trade; and every request the son makes is unreasonable,
if it can be met with the retort, "I didn't do that when I
was your age". Oh, the father's love is unselfish enough, but
it is not a considerate love; it doesn't allow for the son's
having ideas of his own. Whereas the mother doesn't think
of her son as a continuation of herself; rather, she thinks of
herself as existing for the sake of her son. In spite of all the
years have brought, she still thinks of him as her baby, growing up under her delighted eye. She cannot always plead for
him to have his own way, but always she wants him to develop on his own lines, to realize his own character. It is for
that she lives.

You see, now, what I am leading up to. A priest may be a
father to his people, a genuinely loving father, winning everywhere affection and respect, and yet be too fond of having
everything his own way. He has got his own ideas how the
parish ought to be developed, about the sort of pious insti-
tutions which are to flourish in it, the sort of parochial en-
tertainments that are to be got up, the sort of way the church
is to be fitted out. If he resembles the true mother in the
story of King Solomon's judgement, it's only in his rooted
objection to having the parish divided in two. . . . And it's
the same with his people individually; he has strong ideas
about what Jack ought to do and whom Jill ought to marry;
he wants everybody to join his pet sodality, regardless of
whether it's really meant for them, he knows exactly what

prayers they ought to say and what hymns they ought to be made to like, and it's all splendid, and it's Yes, Father and No, Father from morning till night, only—only, you see, it may happen that the parish has suffered from developing too much on his lines instead of developing on its own lines. It may be that some of the souls in it—not many, but some—have been stunted in their natural aspirations or in their spiritual growth by being too much at one man's beck and call.

Don't let me seem to be finding fault; it is superhumanly difficult, especially when we grow elderly, to avoid the temptation of running everything our own way. But bear with me if I try to sketch for a moment the character of a priest who is a mother to his parish, who makes our Blessed Lady his model, not only at the altar but in the parish at large.

My little children, with whom I am in labour again, until Christ be formed in you! He doesn't want the parish to reflect his personality, but his Master's. If he is the rector of a parish, he wants what is best for the parish, not what he planned, what he prefers; that site for a church he bought with so much difficulty, and now the population has shifted in another direction—very well, it must be sold; this new-fangled devotion, which the curate wants to introduce, it was never heard of when he was at college, but . . . the people want it; very well, let them have it. Rector or curate, he directs the souls of the faithful, watches over their lives and careers, with a view to what is God's will for them, though it be at the expense of his own self-importance. Do people leave his confessional, and go to another? He is glad; it shows they have found a sympathetic confessor some-

where. Is a soul continually slipping back into the same sins?
If there is any chance, he works and prays for that soul's
amendment, instead of writing it off as incorrigible. Does a
soul feel drawn towards higher paths of prayer? He does not
try to dragoon it into the ways of solid piety which have
served him; he encourages it, helps it, to follow its own
bent. Some layman in the congregation is a bit too fond of
running things, is always wanting to get up movements and
sign protests; the priest encourages that too, except where it
is necessary to keep the peace with others, doesn't throw
cold water on all the enthusiasm and add one more to the
ranks of the parish Yes-men. You suspect him of weakness?
Well, no doubt that is his temptation. But it is his ideal that
I recommend to you; the ideal of letting Christ form himself in every soul, letting Christ express himself in every
activity in the parish, instead of interfering all the time, at
the risk of hindering.

And what I've been saying will apply—do remember this
—to your preaching. There is one point about preaching
which is all-important, and is nearly always forgotten; you
aren't talking to a crowd of people; you are talking to one
person, the person God means your sermon to help. You
can't give a guess who it is; but you can fix in your mind
the image of a specimen person, the sort of person there is
in the Church. Don't spend your time trying to put the fear
of God into Continental politicians who aren't there, or arguing with heretics who died about fifteen centuries ago.
Choose an imaginary soul that is there or might be there,
and try to interpret that soul to itself; to make it see where
God's will is leading it, what plans God has for it. Actually,

the person your sermon will help will be somebody quite, quite different from the person you imagined, with quite other problems to face. But that person will be helped, because you were trying to bring Christ to the birth in Christian souls, you were not just letting off pious platitudes in the air.

Whenever you pass by the Christmas crib, and see there the figure of our Lady, gazing down in wonder and awe at the life that is sprung from her and yet is so independent of hers, think of yourself as a priest working for God, and remember that that must be your attitude, watching closely every soul in your parish, and not content until you see Christ formed again in it.

Some of you won't be working in parishes, but you will be dealing at first hand with human souls. You will be teaching, perhaps; or later on you may even find yourself a professor at a seminary. If that is to be your work, I think you will see that all I have been saying applies equally here. There is a vanity in most of our natures which disposes us, if we are not careful, to make plans too easily and too self-centredly for the lives of others. Rows and rows of school-boys turning out just like you, rows and rows of divines turning out just like you—what could possibly be more suitable? What could possibly be more pleasing to Almighty God? And there is a much more pardonable kind of unimaginativeness, which will make you want to take your pupils and train them up a wall to be just like some favourite saint, some great man you have known, all one type, taking after a common father in God. But still, you see, it's possible to have too much of that sort of thing. God is so rich in devices for planning out the nature of a human soul; there are so many tendencies and aptitudes in us which are destined to distinguish one man from another, and do already distinguish, if we will look for them carefully, one boy from another, that these hand-over-hand methods can't always be a success. When you find yourself in a position of authority over others, be at pains to study their possibilities; train them, but train them to be the people God meant them to be, not necessarily the people you want them to be.

Or perhaps you will find yourself more of a free lance, carrying out, as a preacher, the characteristic work of your order. Still remember that you are under our Blessed Lady's patronage, and that she wants you to be the mother of Christ in the souls to which your words are uttered. You will find yourself moving about from place to place, always with a congregation different from last month's congregation, and with very little chance of knowing what sort of people it is you are talking to. That fact will bring a temptation with it; the temptation to say the same thing everywhere, or the same set of things everywhere, very much in the same words, and hope for the best. The prophets, you will remind yourself, felt themselves bound to declare God's word to his people, whether they would hear or whether they would forbear; those who rebelled against the message did so at their own peril; it was not the preacher's fault, so long as he had discharged his conscience by fulfilling his embassy. The Sower, you will remind yourself, went out to sow his seed, and the effect of the process varied here and there, not because the seed cast was different, but because it met with different measures of receptivity in the soil. So you are scattering your pearls broadcast, and you are not to blame if there are swine which do not appreciate them.

Yes, all that's true. But do remember, when you get up in a pulpit, that you are not speaking to a crowd of homogeneous units; you are speaking to a collection of individual, perhaps of highly individual, souls. And your business is with the individual soul; you should always be talking to one person. And you shouldn't be trying to pump information into that person, or trying to knock down that person with clever arguments. You should be trying to interpret that person to him or to her self; to develop the seed of faith, to fan the flame of charity, that is in that soul, to bring it to the birth, that Christ may be formed in it. What you have to deliver is not a mere message, but Christ imprisoned in men's hearts.

# 15

## DEATH AS A FRIEND

It is customary, in a formal retreat, to make a meditation on death. And it is customary to make that meditation as uncomfortable an affair as possible; to dwell on all the accumulation of suffering and uncertainty and loneliness and terror which may, which must to some extent, accompany it. The reason for that is, if I may put it baldly, that formal retreats aren't really meant for the sort of people who go to retreats. They are meant for people so wrapped up in worldliness, living so much for the moment, that the bleak, obvious truths which arise from any consideration of man's destiny pass them by. But most of the people who go to retreats do not really need to be reminded about death; they are pious folk who learn a great deal about it from their prayers, elderly folk who feel that it is coming near, priests and religious who spend a good deal of their time going to funerals. Very often they are introspective, imaginative sort of people, who are inclined to dwell on the thought of their last end almost more than is good for them. And I wonder whether it is really very much use to feed our terrors by reminding ourselves of grim details about the sick-room and the graveyard? More especially when those details don't really come into the picture—why should we brood, for example, on the noise which the earth makes when it rattles on a coffin-lid? When it is our coffin-lid, we shan't mind whether it rattles or not.

So I thought we would try to put the other side of the case, try to remind ourselves about the comforting aspects of death, treat death for once as a friend. Of course, it is salutary for us to reflect that the goods we possess, the pleasures we enjoy on earth only belong to earth; that we can't take the goods away with us when we die, that the pleasures are only short-lived. But I think it is also salutary for us to reflect that the disabilities under which we labour on earth won't go to the grave with us either; that the anxieties which constantly occupy our minds on earth are short-lived too. It may help us to get the whole thing in perspective, to deal more confidently with our scruples and despairs, if we acquire the habit—sometimes, not all the time—of shamming dead, and seeing what they really look like. Let's look forward for once not to the unpleasant but to the comfortable side of death. And when I say "death", I'm not thinking merely of dying but of being dead. Although we can only form such a vague and imperfect picture of the conditions in which we shall find ourselves the moment after death, I think we ought to do the best we can; to erect a sort of periscope which will give us some glimpse of what happens on the further side of the ridge which bounds our horizon.

However remotely, the experience of the soul before death and its experience after death must be continuous.

No two people think alike on this subject, and I can see there is an objection which you may feel inclined to raise from the start. "There is one overmastering terror (you say) which, I think, will certainly assail me on my death-bed; I shall be afraid that I am lost. After all, nobody can be certain that he is saved, and the shadow of the particular judgement just round the corner will be the only thing present to my mind. And if, after death, there is any interval before my judgement takes place, surely that fear will loom larger than ever? The comforts and the certainties of earth left behind, I shall see clearly what it means, to be saved or to be lost, and still I shall have no guarantee that I am saved."

Well, I rather doubt whether that picture is true in fact. Somehow, with the weakening of the physical powers, it is not often that a very sick man can concentrate his attention on a terror which has hitherto been so vivid to him; he tends to give up worrying, and to drift with the stream. That may be a danger for some of us; for most of us, let us hope, it will be a mercy. And after death—can we really imagine that there is a moment, even a moment, after death in which the soul, still unjudged, is in doubt of its own eternal destiny? There is only one author in our language, as far as I know, who has really tried to work out these problems, and that is Cardinal Newman in the *Dream of Gerontius*. And he gets out of the difficulty by supposing that time in a future world is measured by some standard quite other than ours. The *Dream of Gerontius* is a sizeable poem, and Sir Edward Elgar turned it into a quite long opera; but the action of it is supposed only to occupy a split second. And the soul as it passes out of the body is already, according to Newman, conscious that it is saved; its judgement has already begun, although the sick man's friends round the bed-side have only just started saying *Subvenite*.

Well, we can't tell whether Newman was right; we can't tell whether there will be an interval, or whether we shall be conscious of an interval, between death and judgement. Even if there *should* be some interval of uncertainty, I think the virtue of hope will be so strong in us that the sense of conflict which it sets up in us will no longer be painful as it is here. No, there may be very holy persons who, for their greater perfecting, are allowed in their last moments to feel that same sense of abandonment which our Lord felt; there may be great sinners who seal their doom by a final sin of despair. But for the rest of us, who have tried to follow Christ and put our confidence in his mercy, I think there will be no room for great anxiety of this sort; before death, the body will be too weak, after death, the spirit will be too strong.

Let us consider, then, first, some of the mortal disabilities which will slip away from us when we lie on our death-beds; which will seem, when we have passed beyond death, so remote that we shall wonder, if we think about them at all, that we ever thought about them so much. What a lot of nervous wear and tear you and I take out of ourselves by worrying; how much, at the back of our minds, we are detained by the thought of dreadful things which might happen to us, or to people in whom we are specially interested, or even to the world at large! Death at least takes us beyond

the reach of all that; events here have no longer any power
to affect us.

> "Duncan is in his grave;
> After life's fitful fever he sleeps well;
> Treason has done his worst: nor steel, nor poison,
> Malice domestic, foreign levy, nothing
> Can touch him further."

But indeed, there's no need to quote Shakespeare at you;
holy Scripture itself points out the same moral, in a passage
of Isaias which is very generally misunderstood. "The just
man dies, and no one takes it to heart"—we suppose it to
mean that the just man dies unpitied, and the text is actually
used with that sense in the liturgy of Holy Week. But that is
not the prophet's meaning; what he is saying is, "See how
good men die, how the friends of God are borne away from
us, and none has the wit to see trouble is coming, and *the
good man must be spared the sight of it!*" All those anxieties
of ours, about the world going from bad to worse, and the
Church being in peril, and so on, do not lessen with old age;
rather, they grow in intensity, because we are out of touch
with our younger contemporaries. But when old age ends in
death, and death fans out into eternity, they cannot hurt
as they used to; we are leaving them behind.

No, do not tell me that we are selfish, if we find relief in
that. The point is, not that we care less about these things,
as we draw further away from the world and closer to God,
but that we worry less. The Blessed Saints in heaven care,
but they do not worry; and the most unselfish people you
and I have known on earth were not worriers. We do not

abandon the world to its fate, with a shrug of the shoulders, when we leave it behind on our death-beds, we leave it in God's hands—where it always was. The trouble, you see, with you and me is that we haven't nearly enough confidence in God's goodness, not nearly enough patience in waiting for him to work out his plans as he sees best; and this unresigned-ness of ours sets up echoes in the nerves which are for ever coming to life and tormenting us. But when the frayed nerves, from mere exhaustion, cease to tingle, and more still when this body of ours is left behind, and we have no nerves to be the repositories of our anxiety any longer, then the whole thing straightens itself out. So far as it is given to us, then, to know what is going on in the world, we shall care still; but we shall not worry.

So much for what lies beyond our power to help: between the leaves of a newspaper. But what a lot of worrying we do, besides, over the things which immediately concern us, with our needs, liabilities and ambitions, with the plans we make from day to day! It varies, of course, with temperament, it varies with our state of life; some people have a great gift for taking things calmly, some people's lives are so much of a routine that the strain of apprehension is lightened for them. But it is true, isn't it, with all of us, and noticeably true with some of us, that our lives have a constant background of solicitude; we are always looking ahead to the next un-pleasant or arduous or embarrassing thing that lies in wait for us. It may be a tough job of work, it may be a difficult interview, it may be an important decision—whatever it is, it looms up on the horizon of the future, and when we have reached the horizon, when we have ridden over the crest of the wave, with a momentary sense of relief, all at once the next anxiety heaves in view; how on earth am I to deal with So-and-so? How on earth am I to get through such and such a task creditably? I don't mean we are thinking about these embarrassments all the time, but they are there all the time, on the fringe of consciousness, and we know how a sleepless night will set them whirling round in our heads, like trees in a high wind.

It is one of the minor consolations of illness, that for the time being we can lay aside all this burden of the mind, and live for the moment. And when we come to our last illness, if we know it to be our last illness, that sense of freedom will be intensified; death cancels all engagements. Imagine yourself to be now on your death-bed, how many important messages would you want to be entrusting to those who stood round you? Not many. No doubt, there will be twinges of regret; such a task has been entrusted to you, and it was well on the way to getting finished; a pity that you should be going out just now, leaving it in the air. . . . Yes, but if it is worth doing, another will finish it, and perhaps make a better job of it than you would have; it is all in God's hands. And this sense you have on your death-bed, of letting go the reins of life, is only the prelude, surely, to a fuller emancipation from all earth's cares, when earth itself has slipped away from you. Gerontius says in Newman's poem:

> "I went to sleep; and now I am refreshed;
> A strange refreshment: for I feel in me
> An inexpressive lightness, and a sense

> Of freedom, as I were at length myself,
> And ne'er had been before. . . ."

He may have been thinking of that sense of lightness which the soul must feel when it is separated from the body, merely in being liberated from a thousand minor bodily discomforts, to which we have grown so used that we hardly feel them. But I think the lightness went further than that; Gerontius had left behind him all that burden of cares of which we have been speaking. And shall we sometimes try to get the better of those cares, which so distract us at our devotions, so injure our peace of mind, by shamming dead? Oh, I know they are not sinful, but they must, in some measure, be our fault; or why did our Lord tell us not to feel them? "Do not fret, then, over tomorrow; leave tomorrow to fret over its own needs; for to-day, to-day's troubles are enough." If we are ever to realize the splendid spirituality of Père de Caussade, by living all the time in and for the Sacrament of the Present Moment, perhaps shamming dead will help us; we shall learn to see those cares as imaginary.

There are other spectres that haunt us and disturb our peace of mind which are sinful; though very often, I think, not so gravely sinful as we feel them to be. I mean the injuries which have been done us by others, real injuries or imaginary, which we find it hard to forgive; I mean the judgements which have been passed on us, unjustly, we think, which our pride will not allow us to forget. We have tried, again and again, tried desperately, to dismiss these grievances from our minds, but always they came back again—with redoubled force, it seemed, as if they were all the more greedy for having been starved so long. Well, on our death-beds it will be part of our chief business to forgive our enemies, and I think under that term we ought to include our critics; and perhaps then we shall not find it so difficult; pray God we may not.

We shall be helped, you see, in that last hour by the consciousness that these things do not after all matter very much; they look very small and trumpery beside the tremendous realities of life and death which lie before us. And after death, they will simply not be there. How much we shall remember, then, of the life we lived on earth, it is impossible to say; memory, as we know it, is stored up in the cells of our brain, and those will no longer be with us. But Newman ingeniously suggests that a disembodied spirit may yet perceive echoes of its old, familiar experience, just as a man who has lost a leg may still feel a twinge of pain in the toe that is not there. If we do remember anything of these earthly affronts, which we cannot remember on earth without a surge of anger, beyond death we shall know that they were nothing. To that extent, at least, we shall be at peace.

We have spoken, so far, only of some of the negative advantages which death brings with it, of the inconveniences from which it delivers us. It is time we should remind ourselves, just for a few moments, that there is another side to the picture. These earthly disabilities of ours grow less, when the cords that bind us to life wear thin; when the cords snap, they disappear altogether. But meanwhile, death, which brings us closer to God, brings positive advantages with it. We are not speaking, now, of the joys of heaven; even the moment after death, with an unexplored Purgatory in front of us, there will be positive gain. And it will be correlative with the negative gains of which we have spoken.

If our anxieties about the world we live in slip away from us, finally, with death, it is because we shall have learned trust in God. Not necessarily on our death-beds, though it may be that unexpected mercies await us there. But immediately after death we shall, I suppose, be aware of it, because we are no longer walking by faith; the time of probation is over. That is why Gerontius' first experiences after death include the consciousness that his angel guardian is close at his side, bearing him along. Trust in God, which meant such a difficult struggle even in our best moments hitherto, has now become part of the atmosphere we breathe. Even during the interval—if there is an interval—between death and judgement, we shall be so conditioned by that atmosphere of trust that there will be no sense of insecurity, though we are still unjudged.

And if the cares of daily living slip away from us with death, it is not only because they no longer concern us, but because we have learned, at last, resignation to the divine will. Oh, on our death-beds this resignation will perhaps be half-hearted enough; we shall fall back upon God because we have nothing else to fall back on, accepting his will because we know it is the only thing we are going to get. But after death, once more, it will be an experience most of us have never had in this life—the experience of really wanting God's will to happen, instead of just saying we want it to happen when we don't. If we have any means, then, of knowing about what is happening on earth, we shall not be asking anxiously for news of some project we were once concerned in. Not because it no longer matters, but because we shall see it now as part of the general scheme of God's providence, not as something which was helped along by us, something which is going to reflect credit on us.

And if our grudges and grievances slip away from us with death, it isn't just that the people towards whom we felt ill-will no longer matter to us, citizens of another world than ours. It is because the love of God will now express itself in us freely and naturally, not laboriously by fits and starts. We shall not, to be sure, make our perfect act of charity until we see the face of Christ in judgement. But the habit of charity, which has been implanted in us by Baptism, will surely have its free exercise in the interval—if there *is* an interval—before we are judged. We shall see the people who wronged us as our brothers in him; we shall smile at the unfair criticisms that once injured us, knowing that they are man's judgements, not his. During that interval, if there be any interval, we shall experience love imperfect, love expectant, but untrammelled in its exercise, because there will be no love of creatures to turn our thoughts away from it. Even if that were all, if there were no heaven to follow, is not the experience of such love enough to make us say, with St. Francis, "Welcome, Sister Death"?

# 16

## TO-DAY

St. Paul in his epistle to the Hebrews tells his fellow-countrymen to "exhort one another every day, while it is called to-day". In obedience to that maxim, I want to give you now a meditation on that very simple subject, the space of twenty-four hours. I don't want you to think of this day in particular, I want you to think of some specimen day when you are not in retreat, an ordinary working-day, and see what considerations the thought of it will suggest.

Almighty God has given us, for the ordering of our lives, an alternation of day and night. *Dies diei eructat verbum, et nox nocti indicat scientiam;* each day, as it were, waves its greeting to the last, bids us pick up again our interrupted works, renew our plans, our hopes, our anxieties. Man goes forth to his work and to his labour until the evening; then night comes, and with a kindly smile puts away the toys we poor mortals make such a fuss over, shuts our books for us, draws a great black coverlet over our lives. So each day is separated from the next by a thin black line of oblivion. As the darkness closes round us, we go through a dress-rehearsal of death; soul and body say good-night to one another. And then morning comes, and, with morning, a rebirth.

Each day is thus a life in miniature. And the very conditions of our existence take away from us that excuse which is man's favourite excuse when he wants to avoid action and neglect his salvation; namely, that we do not know when to begin. *Dies diei eructat verbum*, yesterday whispers its word to to-day, and the word is, Begin. For to-day is unique; it has never happened before, it can never happen again. For one moment it is all-important, fills the stage; tomorrow it will have taken its place in the unreal pageant of dead yesterdays. It has a significance, then, all its own; but this significance belongs to it because it is related to a series. We may think of it as the beginning of a series, the first day of a new departure in our lives. Or we may think of it as one day among others, with the same duties, cares, temptations as the others. Or we may think of it as the last of a series; one to-day will be the last of all our to-days, with eternity for its infinite tomorrow, and it may be this.

First, then, we will think of this day as the beginning of a new departure. How shall we begin? Not by any frantic efforts of our own; we will begin by listening to the voice of God. *Hodie si vocem eius audieritis, nolite obdurare corda vestra.* He speaks to us in three ways; by the direct suggestion of our consciences, enlightened by grace; or by some outside stimulus, a word heard, a passage read in a book, an opportunity suddenly offered; or in the third place through the voice of our superiors.

We mean to hear God's voice to-day, if he will speak to us directly through conscience. Perhaps there are already words of his which we have rejected or set aside, but not quite managed to forget; they still echo in our ears, like some human utterance which comes back to us after a little, although we were not attending to it at the time. His voice has suggested, that in this or that small matter we should reform our habits, that we might serve him better by making this or that small sacrifice. And we heard that suggestion, but said to ourselves, "Oh, well, that can be done any time; I can start any day I like". Yes, but any day is no day, and the only solution of your difficulty is to-day. *Haec est dies quam fecit Dominus*; this is the day when God meant you to start. *Et dixi, Nunc coepi*; the long shelved invitation is to be accepted at last. Or perhaps there is some quite fresh inspiration which he wants to give us, something that has never come into our minds before, whether small or great. We don't want to miss that, but we shall be in danger of missing it, if the echoes of the world are buzzing round us ALL day. So we will try, sometimes, to lift up our hearts to him in moments of leisure, snatched between one occupation and the next; just that fraction of time when the mind says to itself, "That's that; and now, what next?"—that is the moment for a single, brief elevation of the mind to God. In that interval of silence, perhaps we shall hear his will expressed for us, just as a man turning over his correspondence will come across some important letter he thought lost.

We mean to hear God's voice to-day, if he will speak to us by outward signs. In particular, that means that we want to say or hear Mass, and to recite the Divine Office, with attention to the words. God can send a message to us through some phrase which we have recited regularly for years and years, and know by heart; he will let the words stand out from the page for us in quite a new light, if he wants to. But it isn't only when we are engaged in holy pursuits like Mass and the Divine Office that God can make the chance phrase speak to us. I remember once getting a letter from a lapsed Catholic in Australia who said he was coming back to his religion as the result of a sentence, not bearing the smallest relation to theology, which he had read in one of my detective stories. If we will try to live close to God, the whole world of our experience becomes a blank sheet for him to write his messages on.

Above all, we mean to hear God's voice to-day, if he speaks to us through our superiors; we don't run the risk of being fanciful, in accepting such commands as from him. If in any way we have deserved rebuke, we want to be rebuked; if there is any extra duty for us to do, we want to be made to do it; if it is something we shall probably do badly, we will welcome the humiliation which that involves.

So much for what may come any day, God's inspirations; now for what does come every day, our sins. We want, if we could, to make a heroic resolve that we will never commit those sins again, but we have tried, and we don't seem to be able to reach them at long range like that; experience has made us despair of these resolutions. Very well, then, here is a second use we may make of the magic word "to-day". Instead of worrying about whether we shall ever commit those sins again, let us simply resolve not to commit them to-day. *Dignare Domine die ISTO sine peccato nos custo-*

*dire*; let us see if we can't cheat the devil, like some grasping creditor, by saying "Not just yet; not to-day". And let us ask simply for the grace which is needed to avoid those sins just in the sixteen hours that lie between bed-time and bed-time. *Die isto*, let us make to-day a holiday from our venial sins.

This day without sin—as it is such a special day, we will avoid, his grace helping us, those little daily repeated irreverences by which we offend him. And particularly in connexion with Mass and Communion, the daily bread of our pilgrimage. That crowding out of preparation for Mass by unnecessary lateness and unnecessary hurry; that cutting short of our thanksgiving upon some plea of other business; a mere margin of five minutes or so which makes all the difference between treating God as our Friend and treating him shabbily. All those little irreverences, the daily blemish with which we spoil our daily burnt-sacrifice.

This day without sin—as it is such a special day, we will especially avoid sinning against ourselves, by the wrong use of God's creatures. Walk out in the early morning, and look at God's creatures, how beautiful they are, with the dew still clinging to them, and the new sunlight turning them all to silver; the flowers fresh as buds, the air pure, the birds singing as if they had never known what it was to sing before. St. Gertrude says that you ought to offer your heart to God every morning as a rose with the dew still on it. In that early morning air, you recognize that every dawn is a rebirth; nature seems virgin, untarnished, only waiting for your sin, like a second fall of man, to rob it of its innocence. Well, to-day, as it is such a special day, we will try to keep that freshness and innocence of the morning in our hearts *all* day; we will not give in our names to that conspiracy which defaces God's creatures by misusing them.

This day without sin—as it is such a special day, we will avoid sinning against our neighbours. Here it will not do much good if we think about a day spent in retreat; at such times we are artificially protected against most of our uncharities. But think of an ordinary, specimen day of your life; after all, one day does not differ a great deal from another in a sedentary life such as we priests have to lead. You know the people you have to live with; the little faults of manner and of behaviour which get on your nerves all the more surely, because they are repeated from day to day—it may be a blundering sacristan, it may be an untidy presbytery maid, it may be one of your own colleagues. I wouldn't mind so much (you say to yourself) if it wasn't for the repetition of the same nuisance, day in day out. Very well, then, that's splendid; since to-day is to be such a special day, different from all the rest, you won't take any notice of it, just for once; this is the day which the Lord has made, you will rejoice and be glad in it, not waste it in grousing. You know the little unnecessary relaxations which tempt you to neglect your work or your spiritual duties; to-day, God's day, you will not be guilty of wasting your time—God's time. If you are in a parish, you know the tiresome sort of people who will come to the door and want to be interviewed; difficult not to give them the rough side of your tongue, when the manner of their coming is for one reason or another so inconsiderate. But to-day, with this gladness in your heart, you will greet them as brothers, with a cheerfulness which is infectious, which lightens their burden as well as your own. A smile at the presbytery door—how much difference that can make to life's tragedies!

If you are members of a teaching order, you ought to know yourselves by now; and you ought to know your neighbours—an enclosed life has that advantage at least. There is class to be taken at such and such hours, such and such authors to be read, or subjects to be studied; such and such mistakes will be made—with a little experience you know even those. And you will want to be angry with the wrong people as usual; not with the boys who are idle but with the boys who are stupid; not with the boys who misbehave but with the boys who fail to amuse you when they misbehave. You will be tempted to spoil some, to fly into a passion with others: you know their names already; be on your guard, and the temptation will lose half its force. You will have grievances, too, against your colleagues, against A who always keeps his class five minutes after the proper time, and B who always leaves the duster where you can't find it. Then in recreation you will be talking to So-and-so, who makes you want to snub him; to So-and-so, who tempts you to uncharitable conversation. Well, to-day none of these things will disturb your peace of mind, or involve you in any imperfection.

*Hodie eris mecum in Paradiso*, this day thou shalt be with me in Paradise—let us remember that to-day may be the last of its series. When you go to bed, you will wind up your watch just as usual, your letters will be speeding this way and that, assuring your friends that you are well. And then, in the night, just a click in the mechanism of your body, a moment of horror in your dreams; and tomorrow morning the bell will be tolling for you, and your soul will have met God in judgement.

*Hodie eris mecum in Paradiso;* the penitent thief made an act of perfect contrition. He had done nothing to deserve such an opportunity, but he found and he caught the hour of grace. Mercy and pardon were all about him that day, and he gained the first plenary indulgence. Let us, then, to-day, while it is called to-day, hasten to ask pardon for our old sins with the penitent thief. For we too in times past have lived only for the day; we too, like those of whom the Wise Man wrote, have said reasoning with ourselves, but not right, "Come, and let us enjoy the good things that are present, and let us speedily use the creatures as in youth; let not the flower of the time pass us by, let us crown ourselves with roses before they be withered". And now all that is yesterday and is nothing; to-day is the reality, and that day our last this side of eternity. *Cogitavi dies antiquos, et annos aeternos in mente habui;* they are gone, those yesterdays, so brief, so fleeting, and nothing lies before us but an endless tomorrow.

And, as if that were not enough, there crowds in upon us, this last day, the memory of all we have left undone. All the inspirations that went unmarked, the calls that were left un-heeded; all the opportunities of kindness that were never repeated, all the time we wasted on trifling things. *Quaesivi residuum annorum meorum,* we say with King Ezechias; we have looked for the rest of our years, and there was noth-ing left; *dum adhuc ordirer, succidit me,* God is cutting us off from life when we are only just beginning to live for him.

*Ecce nunc tempus acceptabile, ecce nunc dies salutis;* we

can efface to-day, with salutary tears, the memory of those sins whose debt, tomorrow, we must needs expiate by suffering. Let us derive, then, from this word to-day, not only an inspiration for the future, the future that may be so different if we will use to-day aright; not only a warning for the present, to make us avoid this day the temptations that every day beset us, but an attitude, also, towards the past; an attitude of abiding penitence. Let us remember our sins each day, as if we had no more space left for sinning; let us weep over them, as if this were our last opportunity of contrition. And he, who returned to heaven with the penitent thief for his escort, will shorten our Purgatory and hasten to unite us with himself. *Hodie si vocem audieritis*—it can never be too early to begin our conversion. *Hodie eris mecum in Paradiso* —thank God, it can never be too late.